God? Where Are You?

Answering Your Questions About God
and How You Can Find Him

ENDORSEMENTS

How does mankind get right with God, have a personal relationship with God, and receive the promise of eternal life? Sheri Schofield answers this question by simply using the Bible and clearly showing the power of God. I would highly recommend this book.
—Randy Wood—Missionary with Ethnos 360 (formerly known as New Tribes Mission)

In *God? Where Are You?* Sheri Schofield has written a simple, straightforward account of the reason Jesus came to Earth—to rescue the people of Earth from their entrapment to sin, restore them to loving friendship with God, and send them to others with this story of good news. Her retelling of the events surrounding the death and resurrection of Jesus is compelling. It is a powerful story.
—Rev. Jim Stumbo—Pastor, Helena Alliance Church, Helena, Montana

Are you someone who is thirsty for the truth in a day and age when truth seems more like fiction? Sheri Schofield has written a book that is full of truth—God's truth. If you indeed do read it with an open mind to what God might have to say to you, I guarantee that you'll be pleasantly surprised that the truth will, as Jesus said, set you free.
—Trevor Douglass, D. Min., Missionary with World Team

God?
Where Are
You?

Answering Your Questions About God
and How You Can Find Him

Sheri Schofield

COPYRIGHT NOTICE

Cover and Interior Design: Derinda Babcock
Editor(s): Peggy Lovelace Ellis, Susan K. Stewart, Deb Haggerty

PUBLISHED BY: Elk Lake Publishing, Inc., 35 Dogwood Drive, Plymouth, MA 02360, 2020

Library Cataloging Data
Names: Schofield, Sheri (Sheri Scofield)
God? Where Are You?—Answering Your Questions About God and How You Can Find Him / Sheri Schofield

142 p. 23cm × 15cm (9in × 6 in.)
Identifiers: ISBN-13: 978-1-64949-293-7 (paperback) | 978-1-64949-294-4 (trade paperback) | 978-1-64949-295-1 (e-book)

Key Words: Salvation; Jesus; loving God; God's love for us; Jesus's life and teaching; simple Bible lessons; how to know God and Jesus

Library of Congress Control Number: 2021941758 Nonfiction

AUTHOR NOTE

The following stories and teachings contain paraphrased Bible verses—verses told in my own words. If you would like to examine the actual Bible verses, they are listed at the back of the book in the reference section.

DEDICATION

For Heather, who wanted simple answers
to her many questions

TABLE OF CONTENTS

FOREWORD

For those who are wondering about who God really is and why that should matter to their lives—this book is for you.

For those who want to know the main message of the Bible—this book is for you.

For those who want to find answers in a clear, straightforward way—this book is for you.

For those who would like to learn ways to take those answers and make them part of their lives—this book is for you.

With the Bible as her only reference and leaning on her many years as a children's ministry teacher, Sheri Schofield, in a few pages, has successfully explained the great love of God for mankind in a precise and very readable way.

By using the stories from the Scriptures, Sheri has woven them together in a way that makes it easy for the reader to understand who God is and what he has planned.

An extra bonus, found at the end of each chapter, is the "Food for Thought" section, which summarizes the truths the reader just learned, and then how those truths could be applied to their lives.

For those who are looking for hope—this book is definitely for you.

—Melanie Milburn, Bible Teacher with Bible Study Fellowship and Helena Alliance Church

PREFACE

I drove down the mountain on my shopping day, through the forests and fields, into our town, Helena, Montana. As I entered my favorite clothing store, Heather came out from behind the counter to greet me, her face beaming with joy.

"Sheri!" she said, throwing her arms around me. "I'm so glad you came in today. I need to ask you some questions."

A few weeks earlier, Heather was very discouraged. I told her about Jesus and how very much he loved her. That day, Heather made her most important spiritual connection of all. She responded to Jesus's love, and chose to follow him. Now she wanted to learn about his teachings and how to share her faith with others.

On my next visit to the store, I brought Heather some Christian books for new believers that seemed to have simple explanations about the God of the Holy Bible and salvation. But she found them too complicated. Heather was not familiar with church or the Bible. The books used words with which she was not familiar, and she could not understand them. She needed something written for those who had not grown up in church, and who had not read the Bible before.

I had recently written a book for children about discovering God and his awesome Son, Jesus. However, *The Prince and the Plan* did not address adult questions and issues. Heather needed a practical guide which met her needs as a new Christian. I sensed God was asking me to write such a book, for Heather and others with little or no church background, who want to connect with God.

I have now completed the book, *God? Where Are You?* which tells many of the same Bible stories as *The Prince and the Plan.* This book brings adult insights and applications to the stories about Jesus's life and teachings. I have also added some other stories about Jesus which are particularly helpful to adults.

I hope my words will help you find the answers for which you are searching.

ACKNOWLEDGMENTS

I would like to thank my husband, Tim, for supporting me in my writing and ministry. He has faithfully provided all I have needed to do this work. He has always encouraged me. He has been involved in my work to help others understand the good news about Jesus. Tim has been a quiet, steady supporter, and I appreciate him greatly.

My mother-in-law, Dollie Schofield, my dear friend and encourager, has listened to my ideas and has shared her wisdom with me as I have written this book. Together, we have discussed how to present several aspects of this book. I have valued her thoughts.

I would also like to thank my pastor, Jim Stumbo. The good teaching he has provided at Helena Alliance Church here in Montana has greatly influenced my understanding of God and faith. Pastor Stumbo's focus on the grace and love of Jesus has helped me to better understand God's heart, and his vast, immeasurable love for humanity. Pastor Stumbo has given some good suggestions about various aspects of the book that have been helpful.

INTRODUCTION

We're living in difficult times. Many people are lonely, struggling, and fearful. The cry of their hearts is "God? Where are you?"

As I write, the world is held in the grip of a pandemic during which many have died from this virus silently stalking humanity. In parts of the world, there are also great famines because of drought and pests, like locusts. Riots, wars, and intertribal conflicts are disrupting the peace in many places. Besides the health and safety issues cropping up, we also have our own individual struggles, which make these days particularly difficult.

How can we cope during times of loneliness and isolation? What is the answer?

Down through the centuries, countless millions have discovered the great comfort and peace which comes only from God. When people are overwhelmed by fear, sorrow, or loneliness, they instinctively turn to God for help.

During the World Wars, when a combined total of over sixty–five million sons, husbands, and fathers went to war, people sang Isaac Watts's hymn, "O God, Our Help in Ages Past," the first verse saying, "O God, our help in ages past, our hope for years to come, our shelter from the stormy blast, and our eternal home."[1] This hymn comforted and strengthened them. Our one true hope is, and always will be, God. We cannot control the world around us, but we can put our trust in the One who does.

The God of the Holy Bible is my strength in times of trouble. He loves every person on this planet and wants to rescue us from our failures and problems. He cares about *you*. He wants to help *you*. He is real. He is the one, true God. There is no one like him.

All other religions teach that people must earn their way to their idea of heaven or paradise. But the one true God simply holds out his hands to you and says, "If you are tired and worn out, come to me. I will lift the burden off your shoulders so you can rest." *God? Where Are You?* tells who God is, how humanity became separated from him, and what he is doing to bring us back to himself. In God, we find love, joy, peace, and hope. These are powerful weapons against despair.

God once spoke told a discouraged group of people in captivity, "I have good plans for you, plans for your future that will bring you hope, not despair nor disaster."

This promise gave them comfort and courage. Although these words were given specifically to the Hebrews (also called Jews or Israelites), the words express God's heart of love toward all who look for him, toward all who respond to his great love. He spoke these words for you too. He has a good plan for you, a forever plan ... if you want him to be *your* God.

Some, who have chosen not to believe in God, claim our lives have no real meaning. *But something in your heart knows this is not true and cries out for meaning and validation.*

King Solomon, an early king of Israel who had a reputation for great wisdom, said God placed into human hearts the knowledge their spirits would exist forever. This is the reason you instinctively know your life has meaning. You were created for eternity. *God* put that knowledge in your heart.

If you're reading this book, you know, or at least hope in your heart, that God is real and that he loves you. You hope he will rescue you from your fears and troubles.

King David, Solomon's father said when he prayed to God, God answered him. God rescued David from all his fears. He knew God was thinking him all the time, caring for him, watching over him. God was his place of safety.

This is a time for honesty—a time for truth. The truth is *you matter. You are precious to God.*

To help you find and develop a healthy relationship with God, I will share with you some key stories from the Bible, which tell about God and how to find him. The Bible tells us how God has formed strong, personal relationships with countless flawed human beings, just like us. He wants to develop a good relationship with you too.

The Bible tells us that if we look for God with all our hearts, we will find him. That promise is for you.

Before you begin reading, I would like to pray for you.

Most kind and wonderful Father God, thank you that your hands are already outstretched to my reader friends as they search for you. Help them to learn how wide, how long, how high, and how deep your love is for them. Let the words I will share help them to find you. I know that, as much as they are looking for you, you are looking for them with a far greater love. You want a good, healthy relationship with all who reach out to you. You want to answer the questions of their hearts. I bring my reader friends to you now, in the name of your one and only Son, Jesus. May these friends respond to your great love. Amen.

May God bless you as you read *God? Where Are You?*
Sheri Schofield

CHAPTER 1—HOW IT ALL BEGAN

Forever and ever ... before the universe existed ... before there was a sun, moon, or stars ... before time began ... there was God. He has existed from all eternity past and will continue to exist into all eternity future.

Nobody knows what God the Father looks like, because God is a spirit. Our eyes cannot see spirits. But God wants us to know him. For that reason, he told various godly people to write down things about him for others to read. These people were known as prophets. We now have God's words recorded in the Holy Bible.

These words are true.

The Bible tells us God is light, pure without any darkness in it. Just as we cannot look at the sun without going blind, so it is with God. For this reason, God has chosen not to let us see him physically, though he has let some of his prophets see him in visions or dreams.

The Bible teaches there is only one God, but he exists in three Persons—God the Father, God the Son, and God the Holy Spirit. God the Son's name is Jesus. These three cannot be divided in purpose or love.

Conjoined twins sometimes share one heart, yet they have two heads, two personalities. When they do share a heart, they cannot be separated without one of the babies dying. In the spiritual world, it is a little bit like that with the Trinity.

Jesus is the only member of the Holy Trinity who has a body. He took on a human body when he came to earth as a baby over two thousand years ago. The Father and the Holy Spirit are not restricted by bodies. They are spirits. The Holy

Trinity is joined together at their spiritual heart, a great heart of love for you and for me. They were only separated once during one terrible day which broke God's heart. I will tell you about that day in this book.

Each person in the Holy Trinity has a different work to do. The Father watches over all things and makes the ultimate decisions about our prayers, our lives, and our destiny.

Jesus, the Son, sits at the Father's right hand. He was first called the "Word" because the Trinity speaks and acts through him. He now serves as a High Priest, the one who defends Christians to the Father when the devil accuses us of doing wrong. God the Holy Spirit teaches Christians what we need to know and guides our lives. He also reaches out to non–Christians and invites them to respond to God. He is called the Comforter.

In our three–dimensional world, it's difficult to imagine how God can be three persons in One. Here is an illustration that may help explain this mystery. In the Book of Daniel, the king of Babylon had a dream. In it he saw a rock cut out of a mountain and thrown to earth. The rock destroyed the kingdoms man had built then grew into a great mountain itself.

This is a description of Jesus and what he will do someday when he returns to earth and establishes his own kingdom for all people. He's the rock cut out of the great mountain. The mountain represents God. The rock came from the mountain and is made of the same material. Jesus is part of the same purity and holiness as the Father. He was taken out of the Father when he came to earth as a baby. He came as God clothed in human flesh.

God is always good. He lives in a beautiful place called heaven. God's kingly throne is there. Angels fly around his throne day and night calling out, "Holy! Holy! God is powerful and mighty! His glory is found in all the world!"

"Holy" means set apart or specially displayed. If you had a trophy, you would probably put it in a place where others could admire it. You'd want to tell everyone about it. God is like that—set apart. "Holy" also means God is perfect and worthy of our complete devotion.

God is both just and merciful. He looks at the actions of all humans. He knows who is right and who is wrong. He hands out judgments, but these rulings are also merciful, for God knows we are weak. He is always fair, though we may not recognize that now.

God is the most powerful force which has ever existed or ever will exist. Nobody can fight God and win.

God watches over everyone who loves him. When bad things happen sometimes to those he loves and who love him in return, God turns bad into good, in ways we cannot understand or know until we are in heaven with him.

The Bible tells us someday God will bring his throne to earth—a new earth—and live forever with those who love him and believe in him. When he comes, he will wipe away all our tears. There will be no more death, sorrow, crying, or pain. He will take away those things that hurt us. He will make all things new. He will replace our old bodies with new ones that will not die, and we will live with him forever. The Bible tells us this promise is trustworthy and true.

In this new kingdom, God tells us everyone who is thirsty will be able to drink from the water of life freely. This promise is for those who have loved and believed in God the Father, Son, and Holy Spirit during their earthly lives.

There is much more to know about God, but this is a brief look at what the Bible tells us. In the next chapters, we'll look at what God did here on planet Earth.

FOOD FOR THOUGHT

God knew each of us before we began to breathe. He even knows how many hairs we have on our heads. He knows our thoughts. He sees all we do and hears all we say. That is how intimately God knows each person on earth.

This great God wants you to talk to him, and he wants to talk with you too. When you cry out to him, he hears you, and he will answer. He knows all about you and loves you regardless of how much you think you have blown it in life. He is reaching out to you *just the way you are*. He sees your needs, and he cares.

CHAPTER 2—CREATION AND THE SPIRITUAL CONNECTION

The first book of the Bible, Genesis, tells us God is the one who created everything in the beginning. He created the animals, fish, birds, and every living thing on the planet. He created the oceans, the land, the air we breathe. He created all things, including the stars of the universe. As his last act of creation, God made the first man and woman. He called the man "Adam" and the woman "Eve." Afterward, God said all he created was good.

If you look at DNA, which forms the basis for all life, you will see tremendous order and design. Look at a flower. The design is delicate and mathematically balanced. Look at a baby's tiny hands and toes. They are marvels of design. We did not happen by chance. Someone designed us. Someone designed the world around us with all its complex order.

More faith is required to believe these complex designs of life happened by some chaotic chance than to believe God designed the world and all that is in it. *Something in your own heart tells you that you matter. You were created for a purpose.* Follow that instinct.[1]

Everything our designer made is beautiful. *You* are beautiful. God created the DNA that forms your body and mind. In God's eyes, you are of tremendous worth. He loves you. He loved Adam and Eve too.

God put Adam and Eve in charge of all creation. He placed them in a beautiful place called the "Garden of Eden" located between the Tigris and Euphrates rivers. The flow of these rivers is probably not the same now as then, but from the

Bible's description, we know the Garden of Eden was located somewhere between them, in the Fertile Crescent region of the Middle East. Those two rivers flow from Turkey, through Syria, then through Iraq, and empty into the Persian Gulf.

The garden was a place of delight and innocence—warm, productive, and pleasant. It had trees and many plants for food for both humans and animals living in the garden.

The Book of Genesis tells us Adam and Eve wore no clothes, and they were not ashamed. Since the animals did not wear clothes, the two humans probably thought nothing of it.

When God created Adam and Eve, he gave them something the animals did not have—a soul. The soul is the invisible part of us that goes beyond our brains. It's what makes us who we are as individuals. With our soul, we feel emotion. We feel love. We appreciate spiritual things like music and art. We can talk to God with our souls.

The Bible uses both the term "soul" and "spirit" for the invisible part of humans. I have chosen to use the word "soul" in this book because it's a word we use for emotions.

While animals can feel and express some emotions to a degree, their feelings do not rise to the level of human emotions. What animals have is instinctive. They show affection toward those who feed them, or they feel protective of their young or the children who belong to their owners. Basically, animal emotions are about survival.

You will not find an animal that appreciates art or composes music. The human soul goes much deeper than animal thoughts. The emotions of our souls go beyond mere survival instincts. With our souls, we think and plan, pursue education, love or hate. This invisible soul searches for God.

The Bible often uses the word "heart" to describe our souls. While the physical hearts in our bodies will die, the soul–heart is eternal. Our soul–heart cries out for a relationship with God. Our soul–heart cries, "Where are you, God? How can I find you?"

Adam and Eve had a tremendous privilege. God was with them in person. They could talk with God, ask him questions, and express their feelings to him. All this happened face to face with God. Every evening, God went into the Garden of Eden to talk with Adam and Eve. He showed them all the many pleasures he had placed in the garden for them to enjoy. He listened to what they said and felt.

God loved Adam and Eve. But the question was—did Adam and Eve love God? God does not make anyone love him. He did not create robots he could program to love him. Love had to be their own, personal choices. So, God gave Adam and Eve that opportunity. Would they choose in their hearts to love, trust, and obey God or not?

There were many fruit trees in the Garden of Eden. God told Adam he and Eve could eat the fruit from any tree in the garden ... except one. He showed them the tree—the Tree of the Knowledge of Good and Evil. They were not to eat its fruit. If they did, they would die.

Would Adam and Eve trust and obey God? For a while, they did. But there arose a problem that complicated their choice.

In heaven, one of the angels who flew above the throne of God became jealous. He wanted to receive the praise God was getting. The angel was beautiful. Many believe his name was Lucifer. This angel thought he should rule all things, so he started a rebellion in heaven. A third of the angels followed him into the great battle.

The leader of God's good angels, the leader of heaven's army, Michael, threw Lucifer and the rebellious angels out. Lucifer has been known as "Satan," or "the devil," since then.

Satan was full of hate and anger toward God. He knew about the choice God had given to Adam and Eve whom God loved. He devised a plan to turn them against God.

In the next chapter, we'll look at what Satan did.

FOOD FOR THOUGHT

Do you sometimes find yourself longing for love and happiness beyond what you have experienced in life? God created humans with a longing for himself built into them, a longing that no earthly experience can ever completely fill or satisfy. When you find yourself longing for this elusive, hard-to-find love, God is reaching out to you and calling, "Come to me."

King David recognized this longing in his own heart. He said his heart longed for God in the same way a deer longs for water. He was thirsty for God. He couldn't get enough of God's presence.

CHAPTER 3—THE CHOICE

The events in this chapter and the next can be found in Genesis 3:1–13. I recommend the New Living Translation of the Bible for easy reading and understanding.

Satan, the rebel angel, is a spirit. He did not have a body humans could see. To accomplish his plot, he had to find a body to work through. The creature he chose was the serpent. He took over the serpent's body—he possessed it.

The original serpent was not like the snakes we see today. It did not crawl on the ground. It may have had wings and/or feet. The Bible does say the serpent had a reputation for being more crafty or cunning than any of the other creatures. Apparently, it was not unusual for Adam and Eve to communicate with the creatures, for Eve was not surprised when the serpent, possessed by Satan, began talking with her.

The serpent's words were meant to undermine God. He asked Eve, "Did God say you could not eat fruit from any tree in the garden?"

Eve was quick to defend God—at first. "Oh, no. God said we may eat the fruit from every tree here, except for that tree in the middle of the garden." She probably pointed to the forbidden tree. "God said we should not eat that fruit or even touch it, or we will die."

The serpent hissed, "You will not die. God knows that when you eat that fruit, you will become like gods. You will then know good from evil." The devil wanted Eve to doubt God's goodness.

Eve did begin to wonder about God. Had God told the truth? Now she was confused. Whom should she believe? Would she choose to trust and obey God? Or would she choose to believe the serpent?

Eve decided to believe the serpent. She picked one of the fruits and ate it. Her act of disobedience to God was the first sin. We know Adam was with her, standing silently by and watching, while she did this. He watched Eve closely. She did not drop dead. When Eve gave him a piece of fruit, he ate it too.

Neither Adam nor Eve died instantly. However, they did not know three things. First, their bodies *began* to die at that moment. It would take many years, but death would eventually overcome them. Second, their souls had become separated from God. Third, their souls had become slaves to Satan. They had traded their relationship with God for slavery under demonic rule.

Something else happened too. The fruit from the Tree of the Knowledge of Good and Evil began to affect them. They first noticed they were naked. This was not just bad—it was embarrassing.

Adam and Eve looked around for something to help cover their nakedness. The fig trees had large leaves. They picked a lot of those leaves and somehow managed to string them together. They put these cloaks over themselves. If you've ever been around fig leaves, you know how scratchy they can be against sensitive skin.

That evening when God came to visit them in the garden, they did not go out to meet him. God, of course, knew what had happened. But he called, "Adam? Where are you?"

Adam and Eve came out of their hiding place. "We were naked, so we hid from you," Adam said.

"I see. Who told you that you were naked? Did you eat fruit from the Tree of the Knowledge of Good and Evil?"

Adam and Eve nodded. Adam blamed Eve for getting him to disobey, and even hinted it was God's fault. "The woman *you* gave me, God—*she* gave me the fruit."

Eve blamed it on the serpent. "The serpent told me to eat it."

God was sad. He knew what would happen. Adam and Eve's bodies would now grow old and die, but their souls would go on living, separated from God because of sin.

It may seem like their disobedience was a small sin. You might think, "Nobody got hurt. How could that be so bad?"

Here's an example which may help explain the problem. Sin can be compared to uranium, which is radioactive. If you're around it regularly, or if it is in your drinking water at certain levels, you will develop cancer in your organs and radiation poisoning. Having a rock with even a small amount of uranium in your house will kill you and everyone else in your home.

Sin is like that. Even a small amount will destroy the soul. This is the reason God cannot allow sin or sinful human souls into his heaven. Either would destroy the purity and contaminate everyone else in heaven.

Satan captured all humanity. Think of this as a trap—a prison. Inside the trap are all the hurtful actions of mankind—spite, gossip, hatred, jealousy, murder, pride, infidelity, lust, immorality, etc. I've named only a few of the many sins in the hearts of humans.

Everyone born after Adam and Eve was born into slavery to Satan and sin. You may say, "That's not fair. I should be able to choose for myself. This can't be true."

Consider this. The first man and woman were perfect humans. They talked face–to–face with God every day. Yet they chose to go their own way instead of obeying God. They chose sin. The nature of man is to rebel against God. I doubt any one of us would have chosen correctly any more than Adam and Eve did. Their actions doomed all their descendants. Why? Because they were caught in a spiritual trap. Everyone born after them has been born inside that trap too.

Many people think sin is learned—until they have children of their own. Even babies will scream with rage when they do not get what they want. A young child will hit or bite another child, or take away another child's toy. They may never have seen their parents hurt anyone or steal, but they will do it because they have been born into sin. Sin can also be compared to a genetic disease. Children inherit it from their parents. I inherited it from mine. You inherited it from yours.

We were all born inside the same trap with the same spiritual disease in our nature that makes us sin. We cannot help ourselves escape by being very good. We need someone outside the trap, with power beyond our own, to free us. We need to be rescued. We need to be healed.

When I work with young people, I have them write their names on a piece of paper—or take a picture of themselves—and put it into a clear container with a secure lid, then put the lid back on the container. I have them write "Sin Trap" on the container. This helps them to see the problem better. If this helps you to picture the problem more easily, you might want to do what the younger people have done. Keep the Sin Trap nearby as you read this book.

FOOD FOR THOUGHT

Right now, know this—Before God gave Adam and Eve the choice of loving and obeying him or not, he knew they would disobey. So, he planned a rescue for mankind before he even created us. Why? Because God loved Adam and Eve, and he loves *you*. He loves me. He loves the people of the world, and he does not want anyone to perish. He made a way for us to escape the trap Satan crafted for us. God offers to heal our nature.

God reaches out his hand to us while we are inside Satan's trap. If we take his hand, he pulls us out of the trap and frees us from Satan's power. All we need to do is reach out and take God's hand.

CHAPTER 4—GOD PLANS A RESCUE

Adam and Eve chose to disobey God. Satan had captured their souls. Now their bodies would die. Because they had sinned, Adam and Eve would suffer some bad consequences in their lives, consequences which would affect the entire world, both then and now. You can find this account in Genesis 3:14–24.

God first dealt with the serpent, for the serpent allowed Satan to use his body and tempted Adam and Eve. God told the serpent, "Because you have caused Adam and Eve to sin, I place on you a curse greater than any other animal. From this time on, you will crawl on the ground and eat the dust. I will make you and the woman enemies. Every descendant of hers will be your enemy."

However the serpent used to move around, whether it was by flying or by walking, it would no longer be able to do that. God took away the ability to either walk or fly, and condemned the serpent to crawl.

Then God spoke words that were a mystery at the time. They referred to the rescue God was planning. He said one of Eve's descendants would crush the serpent's head, and the serpent would strike his heel. It was the first clue God gave the world about the future rescue plan. The rescue would be led by a descendant of Eve. He would be known as the Messiah, or Promised One. The serpent (Satan) would wound the Messiah, but the Messiah would destroy the serpent.

It was now Eve's turn to learn her punishment. God said, "I will make childbearing and birth painful for you. You will try to to control your husband, but he will control you."

To Adam, God said, "Because you listened to Eve and ate fruit from the forbidden tree, I will curse the ground. You will spend all your life trying to grow food. But there will be thistles and weeds to make it difficult. You will work hard at growing food until the day you die and return to the dust from which you were made."

God looked at Adam and Eve standing there in their pitiful fig leaf coverings. He knew the leaves would tear, and the coverings would fall apart. God killed some of the animals, skinned them and made clothes out of their hides. Yes. Sin resulted immediately in the death of some of the animals.

God knew Adam and Eve could no longer live in the Garden of Eden because there was another tree in the garden—a very special one. This was the Tree of Life. God, the Trinity, talked things over. If God left the couple in the garden, they would eat of the Tree of Life and live forever. Because the humans were now slaves of Satan, they would be in eternal slavery to sin. Their lives would grow more and more wicked as the years passed, and their hearts would grow harder. God loved them, and he would not let this happen to them.

God made Adam and Eve leave the Garden of Eden. He stationed cherubim—a type of angel—on the east side of Eden, with a flaming sword that flashed back and forth, guarding the entry to the Tree of Life.

From that time on, humanity has been trapped in sin and sorrow, selfishness, and evil. God had a plan all along to rescue us and to give us joy and eternal life. He did not leave humans without hope. The Promised One would come someday and save us from sorrow and death.

God would send his Son, the Prince of Peace, to earth.

The rescue plan would remain a mystery until God finally explained many centuries later.

Down through the long years of waiting, God sent people clues to this great rescue plan. He gave the clues—called prophecies—to people whom he chose to be prophets. The clues were so well hidden, even the prophets weren't sure what they meant. The prophets were told the Promised One would be born of a virgin. He would be born in a town called Bethlehem. He would be a great King, and God would put a special star in the sky to announce his birth.

The prophet Isaiah wrote many of the prophecies. The most–well known verses found in Isaiah are a male child would be born to the family of King David who would rule from David's throne. He would rule fairly and justly forever, for his kingdom would never end. He would be called Wonderful Counselor, Mighty God, Everlasting Father, the Prince of Peace. God was passionately committed to making this happen.

God is passionate about rescuing you.

FOOD FOR THOUGHT

When terrible things happen to us or to those around us, people often ask, "If God is so good, why did he let this happen?"

This is the answer to that question. The god of this world is not the God who created us. Because of Adam and Eve's choice to disobey God our Creator, now *Satan is the god of this world*. His purpose is to kill, steal, and destroy as much as he can before God finishes his rescue plan and removes Satan from power. All that is good and perfect comes from the one true God who created us and loves us more than we can imagine. Even God's discipline in our lives is for our good, not for evil. All evil comes from Satan.

We are not defenseless when we love and trust God. Until we are finally rescued from Satan, God reaches out and helps us every single day—if we let him.

CHAPTER 5—THE RESCUE BEGINS

It would be a very long time before the Promised One would come to earth to begin the rescue effort. Down through the long centuries of waiting, those who believed in God kept hoping, longing for the Promised One, the Messiah, who would save them from the power of Satan.

Why did God take so long? The Apostle Peter wrote that God does not measure time like humans do. To God, a day is the same as a thousand years, and a thousand years seems no longer than a day.

Then one day, God's rescue began. This story is told in Matthew, chapters one and two, and Luke chapter one. This amazing rescue plan started quietly. It was not announced to everyone with a great celebration. God simply sent his messenger, an angel, to a teenage girl in the town of Nazareth in the land of Israel. In those days, girls were married around age fourteen or fifteen. This girl was unmarried and had never slept with a man. She was a virgin. She was engaged to a man named Joseph, a carpenter, a descendant of King David. The girl's name was Mary.

According to some descriptions in the Bible, angels are often described as powerful. They shine with a bright light. When the angel suddenly appeared to Mary, she was startled and frightened. Angels didn't appear to everyone. Why was this one coming to her? She felt confused.

Imagine how frightened Mary must have been. She was apparently alone when this angel appeared. Luke tells us the angel's name was Gabriel. He brought Mary a message from God.

"Don't be afraid, Mary! God thinks very well of you! You are going to conceive a Son whom you will name Jesus. He is going to be very great. He will be called the Son of God! He will inherit King David's throne and will rule over Israel forever. His kingdom will never end!"

Mary was stunned and puzzled. "How can this happen? I am a virgin."

The angel told her the Holy Spirit would impregnate her miraculously, and the power of God would fill her. The baby she would have would be holy. He would be God's Son.

Mary didn't blink or ask for time to think it over. She simply said, "I am the Lord's servant. Let it happen the way you have said it will."

Mary recognized this was a fulfillment of one of the prophecies about Messiah. She would be the favored virgin who would bear this miracle child. It was something for which every young girl in Israel hoped. Her focus was on God. She didn't focus on what the neighbors would think. She didn't focus on the possible shaming she might receive from others. She simply trusted God and said, "Let it happen the way you have said."

When Joseph heard Mary was pregnant, he was naturally upset. He thought Mary had been unfaithful to him. They had not had sex yet. Someone else was the father of this baby. Joseph planned to call off the marriage privately. He did not want to disgrace Mary publicly. His heart was kind and compassionate, but firm.

But that night, when Joseph was asleep, the angel of the Lord appeared to him in a dream. The angel told Joseph not to be afraid to take Mary as his wife, because the child she was carrying was the Son of God. Joseph was told to name the baby "Jesus," which means "salvation," for he would save his people from their sins.

The next morning when Joseph awoke, he, too, obeyed God. He took Mary home as his wife. This offered Mary protection. But Joseph did not have sexual relations with her until after Mary gave birth to the baby.

This fulfilled the sign of the Promised One would be born of a virgin. It fulfilled the prophecy of Isaiah that said he would be the Everlasting Father—as well as the Prince of Peace, God the Son.

Jesus later made the statement, "The Father and I are one." He told his disciples, "If you have seen me, you have seen the Father." Jesus was God clothed in human flesh.

Even before he made the world, God loved us and chose us to be holy and without fault in his eyes. He's going to do that work in us! God decided in advance to adopt us into his own family by bringing us to himself through Jesus Christ. This is what he wanted to do, and it gave him great pleasure.

God has loved you from eternity. He sent Jesus, his Son, to make a way for you to become children of God through him.

FOOD FOR THOUGHT

Many people adopt children into their families. When they do, there is a legal process which gives the child all the same rights as children born to the parents. By law, this child becomes a member of the new family. When we put our faith in Jesus, we are spiritually adopted into God's family. We inherit heaven and God's blessings as his beloved children! Apostle Paul writes that, because we are his children, we are God's heirs. Along with Jesus, who made this possible, we will inherit God's glory.

CHAPTER 6—WHAT HAPPENED AT BETHLEHEM

In the days of Mary and Joseph, Caesar Augustus was the emperor, the ruler of the entire civilized world. About the time Mary was to give birth, Caesar sent out a new order. Everyone had to return to their hometowns to be counted in a census.

Joseph, as head of his household, was required to return to Bethlehem to be counted. The distance by ancient roads was about ninety miles. Joseph would not have put Mary on a donkey and traveled to Bethlehem. Remember, Mary was pregnant. The jolting would have started her labor.

In addition, traveling in those days took a lot of time and equipment. There were no stores or hotels along the road. They would have had to bring Joseph's carpentry tools, bedding, clothes, food, cooking pots and water jars, firewood, water, probably a tent of some kind, and food for themselves and their animals—at a minimum.

They most likely loaded up an oxcart—or maybe a donkey cart—with their goods. Mary may well have lain in the back of the cart as it rolled down the road on its wooden wheels. It is possible she walked some of the way, but she and Joseph were probably trying to reach their destination before she went into labor with her baby, so she would not have walked a lot.

When they arrived in Bethlehem, the inn was crowded with other travelers, and there was no proper room for them. They were able to find a place to sleep in a stable, which could have been in a lower part of the inn, or it might have been in a cave. Bethlehem is surrounded by caves, which many people used as stables. But this one thing we do know. They slept in an area used for animals.

That night, Mary gave birth to her son and wrapped him in swaddling clothes. This was a snug wrap used to keep the baby warm and feeling secure. She laid their newborn baby in a manger, a food trough for cattle and other livestock. Joseph named him "Jesus," as the angel had told him to do.

God, who knows all things before they happen, and who is all–powerful, arranged for his Son to be born in the most humble place imaginable. He did not send Jesus to a wealthy family or to the palace. Jesus came for *all* humanity, not just the privileged ones in life. God chose to give his Son a humble birth. It made a statement about his purpose. Jesus came to earth for people of all walks of life, and no one is too poor or too broken to receive his great love. He loves everyone on earth, regardless of their abilities, or social positions, or jobs.

God then sent out a birth announcement for his Son, Jesus. He sent it to some shepherds who were watching over their sheep in the hills. Shepherds were humble people. They tended sheep—and smelled like them. God showed his great love for all humanity by sending this fantastic birth announcement to these humble people.

While the shepherds were guarding their sheep that night, the brightness of an angel from Heaven burst upon the scene. Here's what the angel told them.

"Don't be afraid." he said. "I bring you good news that will bring great joy to all people. The Savior—yes, the Messiah, the Lord—has been born today in Bethlehem, the city of David. And you will recognize him by this sign: You will find a baby wrapped snugly in strips of cloth, lying in a manger" (2:10–12).

Suddenly, the angel was joined by a vast host of others—the armies of heaven—praising God and saying, "Glory to God in highest heaven, and peace on earth to those with whom God is pleased"

Then the angels suddenly disappeared.

Sitting there in the starlight, blinking their eyes to readjust to the darkness, the shepherds must have been totally stunned for a few minutes. One of them probably said, "Wow! Did you see *that?* I don't know about the rest of you, but I'm going to Bethlehem *right now! I'm* going to find that baby!"

"Oh, yes!" The other shepherds agreed with him. They hurried across the hillsides to Bethlehem and began searching every place that had a stable. Finally, they found the right one, the manger holding a newborn baby wrapped in swaddling clothes. After they saw the baby, they spread the word to everyone in town. When everyone had heard, the shepherds returned to their fields, full of joy, thanking God for this precious gift, this baby who would one day rescue them.

FOOD FOR THOUGHT

Jesus was not like other babies. He was God the Son. He was *not* born with a sin nature like those of Adam's race. He would not scream with rage at not getting his own way. Yes, he would probably cry when he was wet or hungry. That's how babies communicate, because they have no words. But rage? No. This was the one human being born outside of Satan's trap. Even as an infant, this child would take all his cues from his Father, God. Jesus was different. He did not have to learn how to be good. He was *born* good.

CHAPTER 7—THE STAR AND THE MAGI

During the events of Jesus's birth, God sent another birth announcement out to planet Earth—a new star in the sky. This fulfilled a prophecy given in the days of Moses by the prophet Balaam about the coming Messiah. He said in the distant future, a star would rise over the land of Jacob announcing a ruler in the land of Israel.

Far away to the east, some astronomers—called wise men or magi—were studying the night sky. They saw the new star. What did it mean? They searched through all the literature available to them from many different sources. Finally, they found the prophecy about the new star in the Hebrew Scriptures, in the Book of Numbers.

A very special king would be born in the land of Israel. His birth would be announced by a star.

We do not know how far east from Bethlehem these magi were, but the Bible scholars think they may have been living in Persia (Iran) or in southern Arabia. We do know the Hebrews were captives in the Babylonian kingdom at one time. The city of Babylon was (and still is) in Iraq. When the Babylonians captured the Jewish capitol, Jerusalem, they took the people as well as the literature of Israel back with them to their country for their own use. If the magi were from Babylon, they would have had access to these writings.

The magi decided to travel to the land of Israel to find this baby. We do not know how many magi went on this trip, but we do know they took three costly gifts on their journey—gold, frankincense, and myrrh.

The magi were not poor. They undoubtedly had servants

and good transportation of some kind for their journey. Camels were commonly used to cross the deserts east of Israel.

Thinking a new king would certainly be born in the royal palace, the magi went straight to King Herod's palace in Jerusalem. Their arrival was notable.

King Herod was an evil and jealous man—hateful and brutal. History tells us he killed many in his own family, including several of his wives and two of his sons. He was a wicked, immoral king who protected his position against anyone who might try to take it away from him.

The magi didn't know this. When they arrived in Jerusalem, they began asking people, "Where is the new baby who was born to be king of the Jews? We saw his star rise in the sky. We have come here so we can worship him."

When Herod heard about these magi and their quest, he invited them to his palace and asked when the star had appeared. Based on what the magi said, it seems this star had burst into the night sky about two years before. This upset Herod greatly. The people in Jerusalem were upset, too, for an angry Herod was dangerous.

Herod sent for the chief priests and teachers of the law. "Where is the Christ supposed to be born?" he demanded.

They told him, "He will be born in Bethlehem."

Then Herod secretly sent for the magi. He said, "The child for whom you are looking will be in Bethlehem. Go find him. When you do, come back and tell me where he is, so I can go worship him too."

By now, Joseph and Mary would have found a house in which to live. They were probably celebrities in Bethlehem, since the shepherd had spread the news about the angels' message. Everyone probably knew who Mary and Joseph were. The Bible seems to indicate Jesus was no longer a baby, but probably a toddler of about two years old—maybe less— by the time the magi arrived in Bethlehem.

The Bible tells us the magi saw the star over the house where Jesus was and were overjoyed. They saw Jesus with his mother Mary, and knelt before him, and worshipped him. They brought out their gifts and laid them at Jesus's feet.

In a dream, the Lord warned the magi not to return to

Herod with the news of the Child's location. They returned to their own country by a different route, avoiding Jerusalem.

When the magi had left, God sent an angel to warn Joseph of the danger. "Get up! Take Mary and Jesus and go to Egypt. King Herod is going to try to kill the child. Stay there in Egypt until I tell you it is safe to return."

Joseph jumped up and hurriedly gathered his little family together. They slipped out of Bethlehem quietly in the night and fled toward Egypt. This fulfilled the prophecy telling how God would call his Son out of Egypt.

When the magi did not return to Jerusalem, King Herod was furious. To get rid of this new king, he ordered his soldiers to kill all the boys in Bethlehem ages two and under. But Jesus was not there.

After King Herod died, an angel again appeared to Joseph and told him it was safe for him to return home. When Joseph took the family back to Israel, he learned Herod Archelaus, a son of Herod the Great, was now king in Jerusalem. Joseph was afraid to return to Bethlehem, a town only a few miles from Jerusalem. Instead, he took his family back to Nazareth, far from the eyes of Archelaus.

Throughout Jesus's life, we can find instances where Satan used wicked people to try to kill Jesus, because Satan knew Jesus was the Son of God. But God did not allow Satan to succeed yet.

FOOD FOR THOUGHT

Jesus fulfilled over four hundred prophecies from the Old Testament of the Bible. (That's the part of the Bible written before Jesus was born.) The odds against one man fulfilling that many prophecies are astronomical—unless he is truly the one about whom these prophecies were written. God knows everything that has happened and will happen. In the prophecies, God described and showed the prophets what he saw would happen. These facts alone declared Jesus was the Promised One, the Messiah.

God gave those prophecies to his people so they could be confident about Jesus's identity. They could put their faith in him. They could trust what he told them. God gave those prophecies for *you* too. He gave them so you could be sure Jesus is the Promised One whom God sent to rescue us.

Jesus said, "I am the way, the truth, and the life. No one can come to the Father except through me" (John 14:6)

CHAPTER 8—WHAT JESUS LEARNED
AS A CHILD

The Jewish people put a high value on teaching their children the holy writings, called "Scriptures." This education was central in their homes. In the days when Jesus was on earth, the synagogues were used as schools too. The teachers in the schools, the rabbis, were supported by the towns. Ten percent of all incomes in town were supposed to go to the synagogues. This money provided for the rabbis to teach, and for them to help the widows, orphans, and poor people in town.

The fathers performed much of the early education of children in their homes. They learned the laws of God and the stories of Israel from the time they could understand. By the time Jesus was born, only Judea, the southern part of Israel, remained under Hebrew control. The people in the northern part of the nation had been taken into captivity and scattered. God's laws and the history of the nation were faithfully taught in Judea. However, because of the Roman occupation, many of the schools were interrupted. Many people outside the capitol—Jerusalem—did not know how to read or write. The gifts of the magi may have paid for Jesus's education.

Formal education was limited to the sons of the family. The girls learned at home. Sons commonly attended school from ages six through twelve. At age thirteen, boys became "sons of the law," responsible for their own actions. Girls became "daughters of the law" at age twelve.

As a child, Jesus did learn to read and write. He knew the laws of God, Hebrew history, and the writings of the prophets.

We know this because he demonstrated those skills and his knowledge in many of the recorded stories about him.

Central to the laws of Israel were the Ten Commandments. God gave these laws to the Hebrew nation to form their government and to teach them how to please God. Here is a summary of the Ten Commandments, which God gave to Moses.

1. God told the nation of Israel to worship only him.
2. God's people were not to make an idol of any kind, nor were they to bow down to idols or worship them.
3. God's people were not to misuse his name in any way.
4. The nation was to set aside the seventh day of every week, a 24–hour period of time, to rest from their work and worship God. The seventh day was called the Sabbath.
5. God told the nation to honor their fathers and mothers. If they did this, they would live long lives.
6. God's people were told not to commit murder.
7. God's people were not to engage in sex with anyone to whom they were not married.
8. God's people were not to steal.
9. God's people must not give false testimony against their neighbors.
10. God's people were told not to be envious and want to have anything that belonged to their neighbors.

These are the basis of the laws that governed the nation of Israel. There were other regulations concerning diet (health) and how to apply the law. These laws were simple and basic compared to the overwhelming number of laws governing most countries today. The law taught the nation how to love God and love each other. The laws were designed to build a strong love for God and to bring peace and unity to the nation.

The law also spelled out the appropriate punishments for those who disobeyed, to prevent disorder and chaos among the people. Within these laws were ceremonies.

While physical punishments existed for those who disobeyed the community's laws, there was also a way for people to seek and receive God's forgiveness. Every year, the people would confess their sins and sacrifice a perfect, unblemished lamb. This was called a "sin offering." The lamb took the punishment for the people's sins. This was built into their religion as a symbol of something God would do, but few understood its meaning. Nor did they know it was a clue to what the Messiah would do someday. They simply accepted this act of worship as something God wanted them to do.

The lamb was offered as a sacrifice at a time called "Passover"—a feast for remembering the time when Moses asked the Pharaoh of Egypt to release the nation of Israel from slavery. The Hebrews (also known as Israelites) had been treated badly. They had come to Egypt as invited guests of a previous Pharaoh. But as time went on, a new Pharaoh arose who did not remember their honored status. He enslaved the Israelites. He made them build the great cities and tombs of Egypt. At one point, he was afraid the Israelites were becoming too numerous, and therefore dangerous, so he ordered the male babies to be thrown into the Nile River.

God sent Moses to confront Pharaoh, and to bring the Israelites out of Egypt. God sent nine plagues against the Egyptians, but Pharaoh did not relent. Finally, God told Moses the firstborn in every household would die that night. To protect themselves, God told the his people, through Moses, to slaughter a lamb and put its blood on the doorposts of their houses, then roast the lamb and eat it.

The Hebrews obeyed. That night the Angel of Death went through Egypt. He killed the firstborn in every house without the blood over the doorposts, including the household of Pharaoh. The Hebrews, who had obeyed, did not lose their firstborns. The Angel of Death "passed over" their homes, and their firstborns were spared. Pharaoh sent for Moses and told him to take the Israel out of Egypt immediately. So Moses did.

The sacrificing of a lamb was the symbol of being saved from death. It also became the symbol of forgiveness of sins. Each year, the nation of Israel celebrated the feast of Passover together, in remembrance of the night the Angel of Death passed over the homes with the blood of the lamb on their doorposts. However, the Israelites did not fully understand what this symbolic act meant.

The Apostle Paul wrote, "This hidden meaning behind the Passover was kept secret down through the ages, but now God has shown his people what it meant." The idea of the lamb dying for sins was a mystery they did not understand at the time. It was a symbol of what God would do someday. The meaning was only revealed later to those who followed Jesus.

By the time Jesus was born, many people in what is now Israel saw the law as simply a set of rules they had to obey. The yearly sacrifice of a lamb had become merely a ritual. They missed the whole point. The law was given to help them learn to *love* God and each other. *It was meant to establish a relationship with God that would change their hearts.* Many settled for just following the rules instead of welcoming this relationship with God and letting God's love flow through them.

God said through the prophets he didn't want people whose hearts were far away from him. He wanted something more like a good, healthy marriage, where love motivates the husband and wife to live for each other. He wanted a positive, loving relationship with his people. He didn't want people who were just going through the motions, living for themselves.

When Jesus was an adult, the religious leaders approached him about the law, trying to trap him into a wrong answer. They were jealous of Jesus's popularity and his knowledge of Scripture. One of them, an expert in religious law, asked him this question. "Teacher, which is the most important commandment in the Law of Moses?"

Jesus said, "You must love God with everything you are— your heart, soul, mind and strength. This is the most important commandment. The second greatest commandment is just as important: Love your neighbor the same way as you love yourself. All the laws and prophecies God has given you are based on these two commandments."

As an adult, Jesus demonstrated his full mastery of the Holy Scriptures' true meaning.

Let's go back and look at Jesus's childhood.

Each year, Joseph and Mary took their family to Jerusalem for the Feast of Passover. We know Jesus had half-brothers and sisters—the sons and daughters of Joseph and Mary—for they are mentioned in the Bible. His brothers' names were James, Judas, Joseph, and Simeon. His sisters are mentioned but not named. We do not know how many of Jesus's siblings had been born by the time of this story.

When Jesus was twelve years old, the family went up to Jerusalem for Passover, as usual. When they had been traveling for a day, they noticed Jesus was missing. They went around to all their friends, looking for him. "Have you seen Jesus?" they asked. But nobody had seen him, so they turned back to Jerusalem.

After three days of searching, Joseph and Mary finally found Jesus. He was in the Temple, sitting among the teachers and religious leaders, listening and asking questions. The teachers were amazed at Jesus's understanding and answers.

Mary and Joseph saw Jesus there. They were stunned. Luke tells us, "His parents didn't know what to think."Jesus, my Son,' his mother asked. "Why have you done this? Your father and I have been frightened! We have looked for you everywhere."

"Why did you need to search for me?" he asked. "Didn't you know that I would be in my Father's house?"

But Mary and Joseph didn't understand what he was saying.

Afterward, Jesus went home with his parents and kept obeying and honoring them. The Bible tells us Jesus continued to grow wise and tall. God favored him, and everyone liked Jesus.

FOOD FOR THOUGHT

Jesus set an example for us with his life. He showed us the way to find happiness and meaning by keeping our eyes turned toward God. When we love God and those around us, we can discover great joy and fulfillment in our own lives. This is not something we can do in our own power, though. Our own self–centeredness gets in the way. Not everyone is easy to love, either. We are only able to live and love like Jesus did, when we commit our hearts to following him. We will not do this perfectly, but with his help, we will become better at it day by day. Jesus is the one who helps us to love God and others.

CHAPTER 9—JESUS STARTS HIS MISSION

Jesus grew up a wonderful man. Because God was his Father, Jesus was not born inside the sin trap of Satan. The Bible tells us Jesus was tempted like us, but he never gave in to sin. He loved people and cared deeply about those in need, the sick, the helpless, and the beggars. He cared about those who were caught in the web of sin and disobedience to God.

We don't know when Joseph died, but apparently, he was gone by the time Jesus was thirty–three years old and ready to begin his ministry on earth. Mary was alone, apparently a widow.

Jesus was trained in Joseph's craft—carpentry—but his mission did not include his trade. His job was to tell other people about his true Father, God, and about the rescue plan. But before Jesus began his ministry, he went to the Jordan River to find his cousin, John, who was also called "the Baptist," for John baptized people.

When a person was baptized (dunked under the water in a ceremony), the meaning was they had turned away from the practices of an old way of living and embraced a new way of life.

God had sent John the Baptist to earth to announce the coming of Jesus—the Messiah—and to prepare the way for Jesus to begin his work among great numbers of people. John lived in the desert, where he spent a lot of time talking with God in prayer. The Bible tells us he wore clothes made of camel hair. He wore a leather belt around his waist. The prophet Elijah had worn clothes like that, too, as had some of the other prophets. There wasn't much food in the desert, so John ate locusts and wild honey.

John's message to people was, "Turn away from your sins. Turn to God, for the Kingdom of Heaven is very close!"

When people wished to let others know they wanted to turn from their old, sinful ways, and follow God, they would go into the water with John the Baptist. John would dunk them under the water and raise them back up.

John told the people he was baptizing them for repentance with water, but one was coming who was greater and more powerful. That one would baptize people in the Holy Spirit. John said, "I'm not good enough even to be his servant or carry his sandals."

When Jesus arrived at the Jordan River where John was baptizing people, he walked down into the water to be baptized.

John protested. He knew Jesus was the sinless Son of God. But Jesus said, "We need to do this, for God requires this of his people. We must set the example."

John agreed to baptize Jesus. He put Jesus under the water and raised him back to the surface. When Jesus came out up out of the water, the Bible tells us the skies opened, and John saw the Spirit of God coming down over Jesus in the form of a dove.

A loud voice from the skies said, "This is my much–loved Son who fills me with great joy."

Afterward, the Holy Spirit led Jesus out into the surrounding wilderness to be tempted by Satan. Alone in the wilderness, Jesus fasted—went without food—for forty days and forty nights, preparing for the coming test.

By then, Jesus would have been hungry. Satan came to Jesus and said, "If you are really God's Son, turn these rocks into bread."

Jesus was certainly hungry. But he wanted nothing to do with Satan's temptation. He said, "No. The holy writings say that people do not live by bread alone. They live by every word that comes from the mouth of God."

Satan took Jesus to the holy city of Jerusalem, up to the highest part of the Temple of Solomon and said, "If you are the Son of God, jump off! You know, the holy writings say, 'He will tell his angels to protect you. They will keep you from falling to the ground or even hurting your foot on a rock.'"

But Jesus said, "The holy writings also say, 'Do not test the Lord your God.'"

Next, Satan took Jesus up to the top of a very high mountain. He showed Jesus all the kingdoms of the world, all their riches, and all their glory. "I will give all these kingdoms and their riches and glory to you," he said to Jesus. "Just bow down and worship me."

"Leave me, Satan," Jesus told him. "For the holy writings say, 'You must worship and serve only God.'"

Satan had no choice. He had to leave.

Then angels came and surrounded Jesus. They provided all he needed.

In the account of his baptism, Jesus demonstrated a practice for us to follow. When people turn to Jesus, they are to be baptized. This act is a witness to others, telling of their choice. Baptism is an outward sign to others of a person's inward change of heart. When we believe in Jesus and are baptized, we take a public stand for him before our friends and family, telling them we choose to stop living for our own desires, and start living for Jesus.

FOOD FOR THOUGHT

Sometimes people say, "I was baptized as a baby. I don't need to be baptized as an adult."

But infant baptism isn't done with the consent of the baby. The parents choose to baptize them—a demonstration of their personal faith. Jesus wants us to take our own stand for him when we are able and willing to make that choice for ourselves. When we choose to follow Jesus and make our decision public to others by being baptized, we express our *own personal* faith in him. It tells others we have turned to God for forgiveness of our sins—our wrong actions. Taking this step of obedience also helps us to commit. It brings us strength and resolve. It tells Jesus, "I am *serious* about following you."

CHAPTER 10—A NEW KIND OF FISHERMEN

Immediately after Jesus was baptized, John the Baptist began telling people Jesus was the Lamb of God who would take away the sins of the world. Two days later when he was talking with two of his own disciples, John again pointed to Jesus and said, "Look! There is the Lamb of God! He's the one who will take away the sins of the world."

John's disciples left him and began following Jesus. One of the men was named Andrew, a fisherman. Andrew returned home and told his brother, Simon, "We have found the promised one—the Messiah!"

This was obviously exciting news to Simon. He went with Andrew to meet this man named Jesus. Standing face to face, Jesus looked into Simon's eyes and said, "You are called Simon. But you will be called Peter." Peter means "rock." From then on, Simon would be called "Peter" or "Simon Peter."

Jesus began preaching about God's kingdom in the region of Galilee, in the northern part of Judea. He began healing the sick and performing miracles. Crowds followed him, listening to his words intently, and bringing their sick friends and family to Jesus for healing. Jesus healed every kind of sickness and disease.

One morning Jesus went to the town of Bethsaida, which was next to the Sea of Galilee. Andrew and Peter were there, throwing their fishing nets into the water. Their family was in the fishing business.

The crowds followed Jesus there too. Jesus saw Peter's fishing boat and climbed into it. He asked Peter to move the boat out into deeper water

Peter was tired. He and the other fishermen had been working all night. But he went ahead and pushed the boat out further.

When the boat was far enough from the shore so everyone could easily hear him, Jesus began talking to the crowd. He told them about the kingdom of heaven, God's desires for this earth. The people listened eagerly.

After Jesus finished speaking, he turned to Peter and told him to take the boat out a little further and let down the nets to catch some fish.

But Peter was reluctant. He had been fishing all night. He and his partners had worked hard, but they hadn't caught a thing. But because Jesus asked, he agreed. Tiredly, Peter and Andrew threw their net into the water.

Suddenly the net was so full of fish the nets began to rip apart. Peter and Andrew shouted to their partners to come help them.

James and John, the sons of Zebedee, jumped into their boat and shoved out into the water toward the other boat. It took both boats to haul in that incredible load of fish.

When Simon Peter realized what had happened, he fell to his knees before Jesus and said, "Oh, Lord! Please leave me—I am too much of a sinner to be around you."

Jesus replied to Simon, "Don't be afraid! From now on, you'll be fishing for people."

One day as Jesus was walking along the shore of the Sea of Galilee, Jesus saw Andrew and Peter throwing their nets out into the water. Jesus called out to them, "Come! Follow me. From now on I will show you how to fish for people!"

So Andrew and Peter left their nets and followed Jesus.

As they walked together along the shore, they saw their business partners mending nets. Jesus invited them along, too. James and John immediately left their nets and their father and followed Jesus.

In addition to these four disciples, Jesus chose Philip, Nathaniel, Matthew, Judas Iscariot, Thaddeus, Thomas, Simon the Zealot, and James the son of Alpheus. These twelve men followed Jesus and learned about God from him. Later, these men became known as the apostles. With the exception of Judas Iscariot, they were the leaders of the early church.

None of these men were highly educated or rich. They were not especially good in themselves. In fact, Matthew was a tax collector, one of the most despised people in the country. Tax collectors had a bad name for cheating people, charging them more than they owed in taxes.

The men Jesus chose had one thing in common. They were hungry for God and for his forgiveness.

Many women also believed in Jesus. They, too, served Jesus and told others about him. Some of them gave money to help pay for the expenses of Jesus's work. Since Jesus and his disciples traveled all over the country, they needed food along the way, and sometimes they needed lodging. Some of the women paid for this through their donations.

These people who followed and believed Jesus helped to spread the good news about God's kingdom throughout the country.

FOOD FOR THOUGHT

Many people feel they have done too many wrong things to ask Jesus for forgiveness. They believe their sins are unforgivable. Peter was one who felt like that.

But Jesus came to earth to reach ordinary, sinful people. Each one of us has done wrong things. Each one of us has had evil thoughts at times. Each one of us needs forgiveness. To help Peter and others understand their value to God, Jesus later told a story, an illustration. It was about a man who loaned money to two people—five hundred pieces of silver to one and fifty pieces to the other. But neither person could repay him. So the man, in kindness and generosity, forgave both loans, canceling their debts.

"Who do you suppose loved him more after that?" Jesus asked.

The answer is obvious. The one who was forgiven more will love more.

If you feel your sin is overwhelming, take it to Jesus, and ask forgiveness. He will forgive you. Your love for him will be great.

God treasures such love. God treasures *you*.

CHAPTER 11—GOD'S BLESSINGS

The Book of Matthew, chapters five through seven, tell many of the things Jesus taught one day on a mountainside. These chapters are called "The Sermon on the Mount." I will mention a few of those teachings, but you can read them for yourself too.

Faith in God was a key element in Jesus's teachings. He told people they could be blessed even in difficult situations, for there are rewards for those who believe in him but suffer in this lifetime. The first few verses about how God blesses people are the introduction to what Jesus said that day. To bless means to give honor and approval. These blessings are called the "Beatitudes." They give us hope in this life, even in difficult times. Here is what Jesus said.

"God gives honor and approval to those who are poor and realize their need for him. The Kingdom of Heaven belongs to them.

"God gives honor and approval to those who mourn. He will comfort them.

"God gives honor and approval to those who are modest, who are not proud or arrogant. They will receive the whole earth as their inheritance.

"God gives honor and approval to those who are hungry and thirsty for justice. He will satisfy them.

"God gives honor and approval to those who are merciful. They will be shown mercy.

"God gives honor and approval to those whose hearts are pure. They will see God.

"God gives honor and approval to those who work for peace. They will be called the children of God.

"God gives honor and approval to those who are persecuted for doing right. The kingdom of Heaven is theirs.

"God gives honor and approval to you when people make fun of you, pick on you, lie about you, and say all sorts of bad things against you because you are my followers. Be happy about it! Be very glad! God has reserved a great reward for you in Heaven. Remember this—the ancient prophets were treated the same way."

After Jesus told the crowd this, he went on to teach other things. He said that when we love and serve him, we become like salt. A bland, uninteresting dish of food can become delicious if the right amount of salt is added. But if salt were to lose its flavor, it would become worthless.

When we have Jesus in our lives and live for him, we bring help and hope to those around us who are struggling. That hope and help is like salt added to a bland dish of food.

Jesus compared us to light also. He said his followers are the light of the world—like a city on top of a hill, our light of Jesus shining from our lives cannot be hidden. People who have lights do not hide their lights under a basket. No. They put their lights up high where they can give light to everyone. In the same way, we are supposed to let our good deeds shine out for everyone around us to see, so they will recognize the work of God and praise him because of us.

People tend to think that outward goodness is all that matters. Not so. Jesus said the law teaches us not to commit adultery—not to have sexual relations with someone to whom we are not married. But the Law of God goes even deeper. Jesus said if a man even looks at a woman and thinks about having sex with her, he has already sinned in his heart. This goes for women too.

How can anyone be sinless when God's law applies even to our thoughts? We can't. The Apostle Paul tells us no one is righteous—without sin—not even one.

We have been born into slavery to sin and Satan. Sin is part of our nature.

That is why we need Jesus so much. Jesus provided a way for us to be clean on the inside, not just on the outside. He made a way for us to come into God's presence, clean and forgiven.

Jesus demonstrated how much he valued all people, not just the men or the most powerful ones. He did not look at people and see age, gender, or status. He looked at them and saw their souls. He sees us the same way today.

One day a group of mothers brought their children to Jesus. In that culture, children were not considered important. Neither were women. The mothers came to Jesus to ask him to bless their little ones.

Jesus's disciples tried to shoo them away. They said, "Jesus is too busy. Take your children away and don't bother him."

But Jesus was indignant. He said, "Let the children come to me. Don't stop them! For the Kingdom of Heaven belongs to those who are like these children" (Matthew 19:14).

The mothers and children came toward Jesus, so pleased he wanted to see them.

Jesus placed his hands on the children's heads and blessed each one—he honored and approved of them—he let people know they were special. We do not know what he said, but I'm certain those mothers and those children remembered Jesus's words the rest of their lives. To be honored and approved by the Lord of all creation was to be blessed indeed.

Once Jesus's disciples asked him to teach them how to pray. He gave them—and us—a model prayer, a general guideline about how to pray in a way that pleases God the Father. He said to pray like this.

"Our Father in heaven, may your name be kept holy. May your Kingdom come soon. May your will be done on earth, as it is in heaven. Give us today the food we need, and forgive us our sins, as we have forgiven those who sin against us. And don't let us yield to temptation, but rescue us from the evil one" (Matthew 6:9–13).

The King James Version of the Bible adds, "For thine is the kingdom, and the power, and the glory forever. Amen" (Matthew 6:13 KJV).

This is called "The Lord's Prayer."

When we set aside time to pray, we remember how great God is and thank him for what he is doing for us. We ask God to help our friends, our families, and all the people of earth to follow his ways. We ask for our needs to be met. We ask God to forgive our sins. We forgive others for their offenses against us. We ask God to keep us away from any temptations to do wrong. We remember God is always in control of this earth, and give him all the glory.

There will be many times when we send up quick prayers for help. We don't need to go through all the topics of the Lord's Prayer every time we pray. We simply cry out to our Father in heaven. He understands and helps us. But it is also good to set aside time to pray thoroughly. When we do, the guidelines Jesus gave are good to follow.

FOOD FOR THOUGHT

Jesus put a special emphasis on forgiving others when they hurt or offend us. I don't know about you, but sometimes I find forgiveness difficult—unless I love that other person a lot. Love makes it easier to forgive.

For those who have given their lives to Jesus, we're called to let the love of God flow through us to others. Failure to forgive others is the opposite of love, which is a sin Jesus wants us to overcome with his help.

King David wrote if he had held onto sin in his heart and not confessed it to God, the Lord would not have listened to his prayers.

We cannot hold onto the sin of unforgiveness if we want to share in God's blessings. Unforgiveness leads to bitterness and more hurt. God wants us to let go of the pain and anger.

Is there anyone whom you cannot forgive? Forgiveness takes supernatural help. It takes *God's* love. Ask God to help you. He will. It may take some time, but keep giving the problem to God. Ask God to give you *his love* for that other person. He wants you to be at peace, and to experience his love and forgiveness flowing through you to others.

CHAPTER 12—LESSONS IN FAITH

Jesus lived at a time when there was no government help for people in need. The religious leaders were the ones who were supposed to look after the poor, the widows, and the orphans. They used the money given by others to do this. People were supposed to give one-tenth of their money or harvest or goods to the synagogues. During this time, most people owned only the clothes they wore and maybe one other outfit. The women in the families made those clothes.

Many people died when there were times of famine, because the government didn't store up food for them. There were some rich people, but most of the population was poor. This time period was not an easy one. People were often anxious.

Jesus spoke to that anxiety. He told people not to love money, for it would soon take God's place in their lives if they did. They would become slaves to money. They would look to money for their security, not to God. Jesus said, "You cannot serve two masters. You will end up hating one master and loving the other. You can't serve God and at the same time be ruled by money."

Jesus told people not to worry about everyday needs, wondering whether they had enough food, or enough clothes to wear. He taught life is more than food. The body is more important than clothes. He said to look at the birds flying around in the air. They didn't plant crops or harvest and store them. God is the one who feeds them. To God, we are far more valuable than birds. Can't we trust he knows what we need and he will provide it?

Then Jesus pointed to the beautiful flowers. They didn't work to look beautiful. God clothed them in beauty himself. He asked, "Don't you know God loves you more than wildflowers, which are here one day and gone the next?"

We are specifically told not to worry about food and clothes. This was a command from Jesus, not a suggestion. Those who do not know God are consumed with anxiety over these things. Our Father in heaven sees our needs already, and he will provide.

Instead of focusing on food and clothes, we are to focus on the kingdom of God, and to live godly lives, trusting God will give us what we need. Jesus wasn't saying we are not supposed to be responsible and work. Rather, we are not to focus on those basic needs. Those who do not know God spend their time worrying about material things. For those of us who believe, our heavenly Father knows what we need. We can trust him.

Jesus said, "Focus on the kingdom of God more than anything else, and live to please God, and he will provide everything you need."

Nearly every day, large crowds of people followed Jesus along the shores of the Sea of Galilee to listen to him teach, and to ask him to heal their sick family members and friends. Jesus taught them about God's ways and healed many. His teachings were focused a lot on faith.

FOOD FOR THOUGHT

In today's world, many people have been consumed with the necessities and the desires of life. Many are consumed with thoughts of gaining more and more material possessions, not on the kingdom of heaven. This desire for more can be like an unquenchable thirst. Focusing on our possessions can dry up desire for God.

We discover great joy when we learn the secret of depending on God to provide for our needs and when we serve him instead of ourselves. Our souls begin to flourish. When we see God as our provider, we discover true security. It is part of God's blessing. He will honor and approve of us.

If you're searching for God but aren't sure about him yet, remember he will always respond to this prayer—"God, help me!"

When I pray those words, I do not tell God exactly how to answer my prayer. I leave it up to him. He is God. He will answer in the way he knows is best for me. I trust him completely.

CHAPTER 13—JESUS THE HEALER

Jesus and his disciples traveled back and forth across the Sea of Galilee, speaking to people in the towns all around the coast. One day they arrived in the seaside town of Capernaum, only about forty miles from Jesus's hometown of Nazareth.

Word spread quickly. A large crowd gathered in and around the house where Jesus was speaking and healing people. The crowd was so packed, those on the outskirts could not make their way through to where Jesus was.

Four men had come to ask Jesus to heal their friend, who was paralyzed. They had carried him to the house on a mat. But they couldn't get through the crowd. Finally, the four men found a way to carry the man up to the roof above Jesus.

In those days, the roofs were often made of timbers, covered with mud and straw packed down over the timbers. When the roof was dry, it was difficult to penetrate. Maybe the men took some water up with them to soften up the mud and straw. However they opened up the roof, they made a man-sized hole right over Jesus. Grabbing the mat, the men lowered their friend down in front of Jesus. They were determined.

Jesus saw the faith of the man's friends. He looked long at the paralytic. As God the Son, he could see into the man's history and current state of mind. He knew exactly what the man needed to hear. He said, "Son, your sins are forgiven."

Some of the religious leaders, teachers of the law, were there as well. They thought, but didn't say, *Jesus was speaking blasphemy* (disrespect for God). *Only God can forgive sins.*

Jesus knew immediately what they were thinking, so he asked them, "Why are you thinking in your heart I cannot forgive sins? Is it easier to tell this paralyzed man, 'Your sins are forgiven,' or, 'Stand up. Pick up your sleeping mat and go home?'"

He looked around at the leaders. He saw they didn't believe his right to forgive sins. He looked down at the man again. Glancing up at the leaders, Jesus said, "I have the authority to heal as well as to forgive sins. I will prove it now." Jesus looked down at the paralyzed man. He said, "Stand up. Pick up your sleeping mat and walk. Go home."

The paralyzed man looked up. With his eyes fixed on Jesus, he suddenly rose to his feet. He reached down, grabbed his mat, pushed his way through the crowd and went home.

The room began to buzz with talk. "Praise God!" someone said.

"Yes. Thank God for what Jesus has done!" said another.

"I've never seen anything like that before!" people began saying to each other.

Jesus and his disciples traveled to another town. The leader of the local synagogue—that's a Jewish church—had a daughter who was sick. The leader's name was Jairus. When Jairus heard that Jesus was in town, he quickly went out to find him. When he saw Jesus, he fell at his feet, pleading fervently with him.

"Teacher! My little daughter is dying!" he said. "Please come to my house and lay your hands on her and heal her! I want her to live!"

Jesus nodded. "Yes. I will go with you," he said.

Jairus turned and pushed his way back through the crowd with Jesus right behind him.

In the crowd was a woman who had struggled to make her way to Jesus. She had a serious issue. She'd been bleeding for twelve years, and no doctor had been able to cure her. She had spent all her money on doctors. Jesus was her only hope. Now she saw him leaving.

"If I could get close enough to just touch his coat, I know I will be healed." she thought. She managed to come up behind Jesus. There. She had touched his coat. She was healed instantly.

Jesus felt some of his miraculous power leave him. He stopped. "Who touched me?" he asked.

His disciples were stunned. "What? Jesus, you are surrounded by people. Why are you asking that?"

But Jesus's eyes kept searching the crowd.

The woman, who knew she had been healed, moved forward, and knelt at his feet in fear. She told him what had happened.

Jesus said, "Daughter, your faith has made you well."

Jairus probably had mixed emotions about this halt on their way to his house. On one hand, he wanted to get Jesus to his daughter quickly. On the other hand, he saw how Jesus had miraculously healed this woman. Jairus probably knew about the woman and her health issue. It was a small town, after all. What Jesus had done was fantastic.

Just then, a messenger came from Jairus's home. He leaned up next to Jairus and quietly said, "Your daughter just died. You shouldn't bother Jesus anymore."

Imagine Jairus's grief. He had set out to fetch Jesus, but his daughter had died anyway.

Jesus turned back to Jairus. "Jairus, it's okay. Don't be afraid. Just trust me."

Jairus nodded. He turned and continued back to his house.

Family and friends now surrounded the house and were mourning loudly, as was the custom.

Jesus walked up to the door with Jairus and held up his hand. "Peter, James, John—come with me." He turned to the crowd. "Stop crying. The little girl is not dead. She is merely sleeping."

The crowed laughed at him in derision. They knew what death looked like. They knew the child was dead.

Jesus went through the door and shut out the crowd. Jairus and the child's mother led Jesus and the three disciples into the room where the little girl's lifeless body lay.

Jesus reached out, took the child by the hand, and said, "Little girl, arise."

The child's eyes flew open. She got right up. She walked around the room.

Jairus and the child's mother were stunned. They were delighted. Their daughter had been dead, but now she was alive. The parents were filled with joy.

Jesus told them to feed the girl and not to tell anyone what had happened.

Why should they not tell anyone? We don't know. The story got around anyway. Jesus had raised their daughter from the dead.

Another time, Jesus was traveling toward Jerusalem from Galilee. He and his disciples were about to enter a town there, when ten men with leprosy called out to him. They were standing at a distance, as the law demanded. They shouted, "Jesus! Master! Have mercy!"

Leprosy is a horrible disease. People get spots on their hands or feet. Those spots would grow and cover fingers, toes, and faces. The spots are numb. Sometimes people with leprosy hurt or burn their numb parts accidentally and not even know it. Eventually, the fingers, toes, nose, cheeks, and mouth begin to rot away.

These poor lepers were not allowed to go home to their families, for leprosy was contagious. They not only suffered physically, but their hearts were aching with the pain of being separated from their loved ones. Those families, too, suffered from the loss.

Jesus looked at the lepers and simply told them, "Go to the priest and show yourselves."

The priests were able to declare a person was healed of leprosy and could allow them back into their communities.

The lepers turned, hope in their hearts, and hurried toward the city. As they walked, they were healed. Yes! They could hardly wait to get to the priests.

But one of the lepers stopped. He ran back to Jesus, knelt at his feet, and loudly thanked him. He was from Samaria.

Jesus asked, "I healed ten men, didn't I? Why has only this one returned? What about the other nine? Has no one but this Samaritan—a foreigner—come back to give thanks and praise to God?" Jesus told the man, "Because you have faith, you were healed." Jesus took his hands. "Stand up."

The healed man stood. He probably flashed a smile at Jesus then hurried after the others who were healed. He could hardly wait for the priest to clear him so he could go home to his family.

FOOD FOR THOUGHT

Faith. It is the one ingredient we need to receive God's healing in our lives. The Bible tells us Jesus is the same yesterday, today, and forever. Even though he is not physically present so you can see him, Jesus is able to see your every thought, word, and action. He sees if you have faith or not. When you reach out to him, it's a sign faith is starting to grow in your heart.

Jesus invites you to bring your needs to him. You may not have prayed before. Don't worry about how you word your prayer, for God the Holy Spirit knows how to present your words to God properly. Just cry out to Jesus and ask for help. It's the starting point in developing a relationship with him. He will meet you there. Trust him. And don't forget to thank him for his help.

CHAPTER 14—JESUS, LORD OF ALL CREATION

Jesus spent many long days healing the sick and teaching people about the kingdom of heaven. One evening after he put in a long, tiring day of teaching and healing, Jesus and his disciples climbed into their boat and sailed out onto the Sea of Galilee. Some other boats followed them for a time. People just didn't want to let Jesus go.

After the other boats dropped back, a storm hit the Sea of Galilee. The waves crashed over the boat threatening to sink it. Jesus had fallen asleep in the back, his head on a cushion. His disciples began shouting, "Jesus! Teacher! We're going to drown! Don't you care?"

Jesus opened his eyes and saw the gigantic waves coming toward the boat. He was not afraid. He simply said to the wind and the waves, "Peace. Be still." Instantly the wind stopped blowing and the waves settled down. Their Creator had commanded them. They had to obey. Jesus asked his disciples, "Why are you afraid? Where is your faith?"

Now the disciples were even more terrified. "Who *is* this? What kind of man could do this?" they asked each other. "Look! Even the wind and waves obey him!"

Why were they so afraid? Jesus had just done something they thought only God could do. They suddenly wondered if Jesus might really be God. The Jews taught people would die if they saw God. Maybe they were afraid they would die. Maybe it dawned on them they were in the presence of their Creator— their God. They began to believe in Jesus more and more.

When they reached the shore, they landed in the region of the Gadarenes. Along the hillside were many tombs—caves carved into the hill. A man who was possessed with demons lived in this burial site. The demons inside him made him so strong, no one could chain him. He would just break free. He wandered among the graves naked, crying loudly, and cutting himself. Demons are evil angels who followed Satan. The demons kept him from his family, from friendships, from love, and from decent shelter. It was a miserable existence, a life of despair.

The man saw Jesus coming and ran toward him. He threw himself at Jesus's feet. Jesus commanded the demon to come out of the man. But the demon spoke to Jesus through the poor man. "Why are you here? What are you going to do to me, Jesus, Son of the Most High God? Please, in God's name, leave me alone! Don't torture me!" Demons can never stand to be in the presence of Jesus. They are afraid of him.

"What is your name?" Jesus asked the demon.

The demon cried out, "My name is Legion. There are many of us here in this man. Please! Don't send us away. Send us into that herd of pigs out there in the field.

So Jesus did.

The demons left the man's body and entered the bodies of the pigs. It frightened the pigs so much all two thousand ran over the cliff and drowned in the Sea of Galilee.

The men who were herding the pigs ran back to the town. They shouted to everyone, spreading the word about what had just happened.

The people ran out of the town to see what was going on, telling others along the way. When they reached Jesus, they saw the man who had been delivered from demons. He was now dressed, quiet, and sane.

The people were afraid. They begged Jesus to leave them. They had just lost two thousand pigs. They didn't seem to care very much about the man who had been delivered from demons.

Jesus and his disciples returned to their boat.

The man who had been delivered followed. He begged Jesus to let him go with him.

But Jesus said, "No. You need to go home to your family. I want you to tell them all that God has done for you and how mercifully he has dealt with you."

The man went back to the towns in Gadarenes and told everyone what Jesus had done for him. It made quite a stir in the region. The man's testimony of Jesus was amazing.

FOOD FOR THOUGHT

Are you facing a personal storm in your life? Are you worried or frightened or sad? Jesus is the master of storms, not just the tempests on the sea, but also storms of the heart, as he demonstrated when he delivered the man possessed by demons. Jesus is standing in your storm, ready to help you.

Right now, focus on Jesus. Ask him to save you from the storm you face, like the disciples did. Jesus will tell your heart, "Peace! Be still!" All you have to do is ask.

CHAPTER 15—A DAY IN JESUS'S LIFE

Another time, Jesus was teaching in the northern part of Judea, still around the Sea of Galilee. At the time, Herod Antipas, brother to Herod Archelaus, ruled the region of Galilee. He was a wicked man, like his father and his brother. John the Baptist had confronted Herod Antipas about his sins, and Herod had ordered his soldiers to throw John into prison.

That day when Jesus was beginning to teach, some of John the Baptist's disciples came to him and reported that Herod had beheaded John, Jesus's cousin.

Jesus was probably deeply grieved. The Bible tells us Jesus was a man of sorrows, familiar with grief. He and his disciples left in their boat and headed for some quiet place, somewhere remote, where Jesus could be alone.

The crowds watched where Jesus and his disciples sailed and followed him. Jesus saw the pain and sorrow in the people's hearts and felt compassion on them. He put aside his own need and healed their sick. The crowd was large. There were about five thousand men, not counting the women and children. Even in his time of personal grief, Jesus cared deeply for those who needed him.

That evening the disciples came to him and said, "We are a long way from any town. It's getting late. The people need to buy food for themselves in the villages. You should send them away."

Jesus said, "No need for that—you feed them."

Can you imagine the disciples' dismay? There were five thousand men, plus women and children. Philip said, "Lord, it would take six month's wages to even give one bite to everyone in this crowd!"

Andrew, always thoughtful, saw a boy standing near–by. The boy heard what Jesus said and held up his lunch. "Here. I will give my lunch to feed people," he said.

Andrew looked into the lunch sack and turned to Jesus. "Lord, there's a boy here who has five little barley loaves and two little fish. But that won't go very far in this crowd."

Jesus smiled at the boy and motioned him close. Jesus turned to the crowd and told the people to sit on the grass. He looked up toward heaven, blessed the food, and began breaking off pieces. He gave the pieces to his disciples and told them to distribute them among the people.

The disciples, their eyes huge, began giving the bread and fish to the crowd. The bread and fish began multiplying. Everyone ate until they were full. They were all amazed.

Jesus told his disciples, "Now go out and gather up the leftovers."

They gathered twelve baskets of leftover food.

Jesus had been teaching them to trust God for everything, including food. Now he demonstrated it. Jesus, the Son of God, provided food for over 5,000 people, multiplying a little boy's lunch.

Evening had arrived by the time everyone had been fed. Jesus sent the crowd home, and insisted his disciples take the boat across the lake. He stayed behind because he desperately needed some time alone. So the disciples got into their boat and sailed away. Jesus spent some time with his Father in prayer, his heart sore from the loss of his cousin, John.

A strong wind began to blow that evening, and great waves started crashing on the shore. Out on the Sea of Galilee, the disciples were in trouble. Jesus knew that. About three o'clock in the morning, one of the disciples looked up and saw someone walking toward them on the water.

"It's a ghost!" he cried out.

The other disciples looked. "Ghost! Ghost!" they cried out in terror.

Jesus called across the water, "Don't be afraid! It's me—Jesus!"

Peter, remembering how Jesus had recently calmed the storm, called back, "Lord, if that's really you, tell me to walk across the water to you."

Jesus called back, "Yes. Come on, Peter."

The other disciples watched in amazement and fear as Peter climbed out of the boat, his eyes fixed on Jesus. He must have felt a great thrill at first. He was walking on water too. Then he took his eyes off Jesus and looked at the giant waves coming toward him. Suddenly, Peter was terrified. He began to sink into the water.

"Lord! Save me!" he screamed in fear.

Jesus was instantly beside Peter, grasping his hands and hauling him out of the water. He held onto Peter and scolded gently. "You have so little faith. Why did you doubt?" He led Peter over to the boat, walking with him on the water, an arm around Peter to keep him from slipping back into the waves. Together, they climbed back into the boat. As soon as they were in the boat, the wind stopped, and the storm died down.

Jesus's disciples bowed down to Jesus and declared, "You are truly the Son of God!"

FOOD FOR THOUGHT

Did Peter have little faith? Yes. His faith was small. But even a small amount of faith helped him walk on water for a few steps. What about the other disciples? They had all stayed in the boat and didn't even ask to walk on water with Jesus. Though Peter's faith was small, he believed more strongly than the other disciples did. Jesus would gradually teach his followers to have great faith. He wants to teach us faith too. Faith and trust aren't something we learn all at once. We take baby steps at first. Little by little, our faith grows.

If you're struggling with fear or anxiety, cry out to Jesus like Peter did. "Lord, save me!" Let Jesus fill you with his peace. Trust him and see what he will do for you.

CHAPTER 16—JESUS TO THE RESCUE

Abraham, whose name was once Abram, was the father of the Hebrew nation—the Israelite people. Abraham was a man who had great faith in God and loved him deeply. He lived in Ur of the Chaldees, a city in what is now southern Iraq. Most of the inhabitants didn't worship the one true God. They worshipped things God created. This may have been why God asked Abram to leave Ur.

God told Abraham to leave his home country and his relatives and to go to a land God would show him. God said, "I will make a great nation from you. I will bless you and make you famous. You will bring my blessing to others. I will honor those who honor you. I will curse those who treat you with contempt. Through you, all nations of the world will be blessed.'"

This blessing is known as the Abrahamic Covenant. A covenant is a contract. In these verses is hidden one of the clues—a prophecy—about the Promised One. It also clearly tells the Hebrew people they will be a blessing to others.

Somewhere along the way, many of the religious leaders had completely forgotten that part of the contract between Abram and God. Many became power–hungry and threw their weight around, not caring whom they hurt. They did not bless the nations around them, let alone their own people.

By the time Jesus came on the scene, many of the religious leaders were using the Law of Moses to their own advantage and were being merciless to those whom they saw as their inferiors. They were tremendously jealous of Jesus. He was drawing huge crowds of people. These people were hanging on every word Jesus said. The crowds were calling Jesus the Messiah.

The hardcore religious leaders sent their soldiers to arrest Jesus, but the Temple guards came back without him. They said they had never heard anyone speak like this man. They were impressed.

The religious leaders tried to trip up Jesus, using the Law of Moses as their weapon. If they could just catch him disobeying the law, they could arrest him.

One day Jesus was teaching in the Temple. A large crowd came to hear him speak. While Jesus was talking, the religious leaders dragged a woman into the Temple area and threw her at Jesus's feet.

"This woman was caught in the act of having sex with a man to whom she was not married!" they said. "According to the Law of Moses, we're supposed to stone her. What about it, Jesus? What do you say?"

They knew of Jesus's compassion for people. He had often condemned the religious leaders, but he had shown mercy to the common people. Would he side with this woman? If he didn't agree to stone her, he would be in trouble with the law, and they could destroy him. If he did agree, and they stoned the woman, people might turn away from Jesus. They thought they'd devised the perfect trap.

Jesus was sitting while he taught, as was the custom. He looked at those religious men. They had not brought the man involved in the affair, only the woman. He knew their hard hearts. They did not love God. They did not love the people they were supposed to serve. They loved only their own power and position. They didn't care about that woman in the least. They had no compassion.

Jesus leaned over and began writing in the dust on the floor with his finger.

The religious leaders kept shouting, "Shall we stone her? What do you say?"

What was Jesus writing? We do not know. Maybe he was writing the sins of the religious leaders in the dust. Maybe he was writing the names of the women those religious leaders had slept with unlawfully. Whatever he was writing, the words got to those leaders.

Jesus stood up and looked into their eyes. "Let the one who has never sinned throw the first stone." Then he leaned down and continued writing in the dust.

When the accusers heard this, they hung their heads and, one by one, beginning with the oldest, they left. Then Jesus stood up again and said to the woman, "Where are those who accused you? Didn't even one of them stay to condemn you?"

"No, Lord," she said.

Jesus said, "Neither do I. Go. And do not sin anymore."

Jesus gave the woman a second chance to get her heart right with God before it was too late. There is no doubt in my mind this woman followed Jesus with great devotion after that. He had saved her life. I believe he also saved her soul, though the Bible does not tell us what happened later.

John writes that Jesus's purpose in coming was to show us God the Father's love. "For this is how God loved the world: He gave his one and only Son, so that everyone who believes in him will not perish but have eternal life. God sent his Son into the world not to judge the world, but to save the world through him" (John 3: 16—17).

What does it mean to perish? The Bible describes perishing in more than one way, but basically, to perish is to be separated from God and all that he is—separated from his goodness, love, beauty, joy, peace—existing in misery, without hope—forever. Those who choose to go their own way instead of following Jesus during their lifetime will have no more chances to live in heaven with God after they die. God does not want that to happen. He wants to rescue each one of us.

If we do choose to follow Jesus, who was God in human flesh, our eternity with him in heaven is certain. Jesus said, "I am the way, the truth, and the life. No one can come to the Father except through me" (John 14:6).

Jesus came to give us a spiritually healthy, satisfying life in this world, and an eternity with God after this life passes. He loved that woman, just as he loves you and me. He gave her another chance to turn toward him in faith. He gave her an opportunity to choose life. I believe she did.

FOOD FOR THOUGHT

The Law of Moses was given to teach people to love God with all their hearts, and to love their neighbors as themselves.

Even with the law before them, drilled into their heads day after day, nobody was able to keep it perfectly.

The reason? We are all born into slavery to Satan. We are caught in Satan's trap of sin. Jesus came to get us out of that trap, not to condemn us. He offers us a choice of where *we* want to spend eternity—with God or without him. We can choose life with God by faith, by believing what Jesus has told us in the Bible. When we choose God, he delivers us from Satan's sin trap and begins a good work in us. Jesus gives us this opportunity at eternal life spent with God because he loves us.

CHAPTER 17—UNCONDITIONAL LOVE

To illustrate God's love for us, Jesus told a parable, a story to teach a lesson.

A man with a lot of land and servants had two sons. The younger son was impatient with life on the ranch. He told his dad, "I want you to give me my inheritance now. I'm young. I want to enjoy life and not wait around for you to die before I inherit your money."

The father divided his wealth and gave half of it to the younger son, and the young man went off to the city. There he spent his entire inheritance on wild living and parties with his friends. When the money ran out, his friends deserted him. The man looked around for work. All he could find was a job as a servant feeding the pigs belonging to a rich man. He was so hungry he even ate some of the food thrown out to the pigs.

One day he looked around and realized what he had done. He thought, *The hired servants in my father's house have more than this. They have plenty of food. Yet here I am starving, eating the pigs' food. I should go home. I'll say, 'Father, I have sinned against you and against God. I'm not worthy of being called your son. Please hire me as one of your servants.'*

He left the pigs and headed home.

Meanwhile, his father looked down the road every day, hoping his son would return. One day as he looked, he saw his son off in the distance. His heart was suddenly bursting with love and compassion. He raced down the road and threw his arms around the young man.

"Father, I've sinned against you and against God. I'm not worthy to even be called your son." He didn't get any further than that.

His father called out to his servants, "'Hurry! Go get the best clothes in the house and put them on my son. Bring him a ring and shoes. Go kill that calf we have been fattening up and butcher it for dinner. We're going to have a feast to celebrate. My son, whom I thought was dead, has come back! I thought we had lost him, but now he's back." They had a great feast and everyone celebrated.

Not the older brother though. He was angry his dad welcomed his brother back. He said, "Dad, why are you doing this? My brother wasted all his money, and you throw him a party? I've been serving you here at home all these years, and I've never had a party like this."

The father said, "Son, yes, you have always been here with me, and you're going to inherit everything I have. But today is a time of rejoicing. Be happy and celebrate! Your brother is home! I thought we had lost him—I feared he might be dead—but now he is back."

FOOD FOR THOUGHT

Jesus told this parable to illustrate how much God loves each one of us, even when we've blown it. He holds out his arms and invites us to come to him. We may not have the strength in ourselves to break away from the mess we've managed to get into, but God does. He can rescue us. He can help us break free from the things dragging us into slavery. He can and will restore everyone who comes to him through Jesus. With God, all things are possible.

CHAPTER 18—JESUS AND LAZARUS

A family in the town of Bethany, not far from Jerusalem, were great friends with Jesus. Their names were Martha, Mary, and Lazarus.

Lazarus became ill one day when Jesus was about a two-day walk away from them. The two sisters sent a messenger to Jesus. The messenger said, "Lord, Lazarus, your friend whom you love, is very sick."

When Jesus heard about it, he said, "His sickness will not end in death. It has happened to bring glory to God and for the Son of God's glory."

Jesus sent this message back to Mary and Martha. Even though he loved and cared about them, he did not return with the messenger. Instead, he stayed where he was for two more days, teaching crowds of people and healing them. Jesus then told his disciples they were going back to Judea.

The last time Jesus and his disciples had been in Judea, the religious leaders had tried to kill Jesus by throwing stones at him. The disciples protested about returning. "Teacher, why are you doing this? Don't you remember what happened last time we were there? They were trying to kill you. Why are we going back now?"

Jesus told them Lazarus had fallen asleep. Jesus was going back to Bethany to awaken him.

The disciples were puzzled. If Lazarus was sick, then sleep would make him better. Why would Jesus want to wake him?

Jesus saw he needed to speak plainly. He told them Lazarus was dead. He said he was glad they were not there, because now they would truly believe in him. They needed to go to Judea now. Can you imagine that? There were still some disciples who did not really believe Jesus was the Son of God, even though they had witnessed his many miracles.

The disciples were not at all happy about this.

Thomas, nicknamed the Twin, said to his fellow disciples, "Well, we might as well go along and die with him." Cynical. Unbelieving. But he was brave in the face of certain danger.

By the time Jesus and his disciples reached Bethany, Lazarus had been dead for four days and was already in his grave. Many of the family's friends who lived in Jerusalem, plus their friends in Bethany, had come to comfort Mary and Martha. They were all crying together over this great loss.

Someone told Mary and Martha, "Look. There's Jesus. He's coming down the road now."

Martha stood, sighed, and hurried down the road to meet him. But Mary didn't want to go with her. She stayed behind with her friends.

Martha said to Jesus, "Lord, if only you had been here, Lazarus would not have died." She shook her head sadly. "But I know, even now, that God will give you whatever you ask."

Jesus told her, "Lazarus will live again, Martha."

"Yes," Martha said, "I know about the resurrection. Lazarus will rise along with everyone else on resurrection day."

Jesus said, "Martha, *I am the resurrection and the life.* Anyone who believes in me will live, even after dying. Everyone who lives in me and believes in me will never ever die. Do you believe this, Martha?"

"Yes, Lord," she told him. "I have always believed you are the Messiah, the Son of God the one who has come into the world from God" (John 11:25–27, italic added).

Did she truly believe that? Or was she only being polite? Her underlying anger at Jesus indicates she did not truly believe yet. She turned back to the house, looking for Mary.

When Martha found Mary, she told her Jesus had come, and he wanted to see her.

Mary went out to where Jesus stood waiting. Those who were at the house to comfort the two sisters assumed Mary was going to the tomb where Lazarus lay so she could grieve. They followed her at a distance, wanting to be of comfort.

When Mary reached Jesus, she repeated what Martha had said. "Lord, if you had been here, Lazarus would not have died." She was upset at Jesus too.

Jesus saw Mary's tears and swollen eyes. He asked where they had put Lazarus's body.

"Come. We'll show you," people in the crowd said. But among themselves, they were criticizing Jesus. Some said, "Jesus has healed so many others. He even healed a blind man. Why didn't he come in time to heal Lazarus? Why did he let Lazarus die?"

Jesus knew their thoughts and was troubled. Can you imagine how he must have felt? Even his disciples and dearest friends didn't believe in him fully. He had spent three years demonstrating his power over all of creation. He had fed large crowds with only a few loaves and fish, multiplying the meager supplies thousands of times over. He had walked on water and stilled the storms. He had cast out demons. He had raised others from the dead. Why couldn't they believe he could raise Lazarus, even four days after Lazarus had died? Jesus had come to save people. But they couldn't be saved unless they believed in him.

They finally came to the tomb. In those days, family tombs were caves with large stones in front that could be rolled across the opening.

The Bible tells us Jesus wept.

The crowd thought Jesus was weeping because he had loved Lazarus so much and was sad Lazarus had died. But was he? Jesus knew what he was about to do. Was he really weeping because his friend had died? Or was he grieved that Mary and Martha, his dear friends, were suffering so much because they did not have faith enough to trust him? All we know for sure is Jesus let Lazarus die in order teach his disciples to believe in him, to trust him. And we know Jesus wept.

Jesus stepped up to the tomb. "Roll the stone away," he ordered.

"No, Jesus," Martha protested. "He has been dead for four days now. It's going to smell awful." She clearly didn't believe in Jesus's power.

Jesus responded. "Didn't I say you would see God's glory if you would only believe?" (John 11:40). Some of the stronger men in the crowd rolled the stone away from the tomb's entrance.

Jesus looked up to heaven and said, "Father, thank you for hearing me. You always hear me, but I said it out loud for the sake of all these people standing here, so they will believe you sent me." Then Jesus shouted, "Lazarus, come out here!"

Everyone held their breath, eyes opened wide as they stared into the dark cave. Suddenly, there he was. Lazarus, wrapped in heavy swaths of grave clothes and spices, was struggling toward the entrance of the cave.

Jesus said, "Unwrap him. Let him go."

Lazarus's sisters and their friends hurried to help him, no doubt blown away by this miracle, and took away the heavy layers of cloth around his body.

Many now believed in Jesus. They had heard Jesus had power, but raising someone from the dead after he had been dead for four whole days? Wow!

Some of the people hurried back to Jerusalem to tell everyone about this incredible miracle.

But the religious leaders in Jerusalem became even more upset. "This isn't good. What can we do to stop this man? He's performing miracles, and if we let him, everyone is going to believe and follow him. The Romans here in Jerusalem won't like it. They'll tell Caesar, and he will send his army to destroy our Temple and this entire country."

Those leaders chose not to believe in Jesus, not even when they saw his great power. It did not matter to them that Jesus was sent from God. He threatened their power. Jealousy filled their hearts. Fear of the Romans, who had conquered their land and now ruled over them, only amplified their unbelief. They had no faith in God, who sent Jesus to them.

The high priest, Caiaphas, finally said, "You don't realize it is better for you that one man should die for the people than for the whole nation to be destroyed" (John 11:50). When he said that, he did not know his words would lead to the fulfillment of God's rescue plan for all mankind. He didn't think up those words on his own. God put them on his lips to point ahead, to fulfill prophecy. From that day on, the religious leaders looked for a way to kill Jesus.

FOOD FOR THOUGHT

Has there ever been a time in your life when you were afraid you would die, but then you were suddenly spared? Someone might have said, "That was a miracle."

God sometimes steps in and does a miracle to let you know he loves you, and he is there for you. Even small miracles are a sign of his great power. Did you chalk an experience up to coincidence? Or luck? Or did you believe in the miracle?

God is the great miracle worker. He was reaching out to you with his great love. Did you accept that miracle as coming from him?

CHAPTER 19—JESUS NEARS HIS FINAL WEEK

Jesus did many more miracles than I have recorded so far in this book. The Apostle John wrote, "Jesus also did many other things. If they were all written down, I suppose the whole world could not contain the books that would be written" (John 21:25). I have given you a sample of what Matthew, Mark, Luke, and John wrote in the books named after them in the Bible. Matthew and John were eyewitnesses of these miracles. Mark and Luke may have seen some of the miracles and written down what they had seen and what some of the other eyewitnesses said.

The most important work Jesus did followed his miracles of feeding the multitudes, healing their diseases, and raising people from the dead. His greatest work of all was yet to come.

Jesus had supper one night at the home of Lazarus, whom he had raised from the dead, and his sisters Mary and Martha. The feast was in Jesus's honor.

During the feast, Mary took a jar of costly perfume made from essence of nard, anointed Jesus's feet, and wiped his feet with her hair.

The fragrance filled the room. Everyone looked at Mary. "What?" said some of the disciples. "Why did she do that? If she had given us the ointment, we could have sold it and given the money to the poor." They were indignant.

But Jesus said, "Leave her alone. What she did was beautiful. There will always be poor people for you to feed, but you will not have me with you forever. Mary was preparing me for my burial. In the future, wherever you tell the good news

I have brought, you must also tell the story of what Mary did today." Jesus saw into Mary's heart. He knew her motive in anointing him.

Mary was probably the only one who had been truly listening to what Jesus was saying. She seemed to understand Jesus would be killed. But did she know all he would do for her through his death? Maybe she did. The Bible tells us she sat at Jesus's feet and listened. She may have heard about Jesus's words to one of his followers, Nicodemus. Jesus had said, "And as Moses lifted up the bronze snake on a pole in the wilderness, so the Son of Man must be lifted up" (John 3:14).

Jesus was referring to a time when Moses led Israel out of slavery in Egypt. From Egypt to the land of Canaan, which later became known as the land of Israel, was a long journey. The Israelites had to walk through the wilderness where there was no food. God sent a special food called "manna" from the skies each night. Manna was white flakes that tasted like honey cakes. When they were thirsty, God brought them water from rocks in the desert. Despite this, the people became impatient and began saying bad things about God and Moses.

"Why did you bring us out of Egypt just to die here in the wilderness?" they complained. "There isn't anything to eat out here, and nothing to drink, and this manna stuff tastes terrible!"

They were so ungrateful for God's miracles that God sent poisonous snakes to their encampment. Many people were bitten and they died. The people were frightened. They knew God was angry with them for their complaints against him and against Moses. They went to Moses said, "We admit it— we have sinned when we complained about God and you. Please pray to him and ask God to take away the snakes." Then Moses prayed for the people.

Then God told him, "I want you to make a serpent (snake) out of bronze. Make it look like the ones in camp. Then put it up on a pole so everyone can see. Everyone who has been bitten will live—if they just look at it."

Moses followed the instructions. He made a snake out of bronze and attached it to a pole. The pole would probably have had been constructed like a cross in order to hold the snake up.

The people crowded around the bronze snake. Whenever anyone looked up at the serpent, they were healed. They lived.

Jesus said he would become just like that bronze serpent, which represented sin and death. Mary may not have seen the full significance of what Jesus said, but she did know this much—her beloved Jesus would die. Her heart was breaking. The others did not yet know what the future held. Out of her great love for Jesus, Mary spent a fortune on him when she poured out the perfume. Her action told everyone she loved Jesus, who would soon lay down his life to bring eternal life to the world, for all who believe.

Jesus's disciples still thought Jesus would be made king of the Jews soon and would force the Romans out of their country. They were remembering the prophecies about the Messiah, which said he would come as a great king. Both prophecies were true—the prophecy about Jesus's dying for our sins and the prophecy of him coming as King. But they were to happen at different times.

Prophecies can be a lot like mountain ranges. Much of the time, they look like a single line of tall mountains in the distance. However, in the early morning, with the mists rising from the forests, you see there are several smaller mountains between the highest peak and the area closest to you. In the same way, several prophecies had to be fulfilled before the final triumph when Jesus would become king.

Shortly after Jesus raised Lazarus from the dead and dined with Simon, he told his disciples to borrow a donkey colt for him. He rode this donkey toward Jerusalem, fulfilling a prophecy given by the prophet Zechariah. "Rejoice, O people of Zion! Shout in triumph, O people of Jerusalem! Look, your king is coming to you. He is righteous and victorious, yet he is humble, riding on a donkey—riding on a donkey's colt" (Zechariah 9:9).

The people recognized what Jesus was doing. He was their king. He was their Messiah—the Promised One. Some of the people took off their coats and spread them on the road or broke off palm branches, throwing some on the ground for the donkey to walk over. They shouted, "Hosanna to the Son of David! Blessed is he who comes in the name of the Lord!"

(Matthew 21:9). What did those words mean? "Hosanna" means "save" or "save now". Saying Jesus was the Son of David was recognizing him as Messiah. In our words, they would be saying, "Save now, Messiah! Honor and approval to the one who comes in the name of the Lord."

Everyone in Jerusalem was wondering what was going on. They asked the crowd around Jesus, "Who is this?" The people said, "It's Jesus! You know—the prophet from Nazareth!"

Jesus rode up to the Temple at the top of the hill. Inside, people were selling animals for sacrifices. It was nearing the time of the Passover feast with its animal sacrifices. Jewish people came from all over the civilized world to worship God in Jerusalem. They couldn't bring their own livestock for the offerings if they came from a distance. The merchants in Jerusalem took advantage of them. They charged as much as they could get for the animals and cheated the visitors when they traded their money for Jerusalem coin.

The stench from animal excrement filled the air. People shouted and haggled over the animals. This was done in the part of the Temple where non–Jews came to learn about God and to pray.

Jesus grew angry. He braided a whip out of rope and began driving the moneychangers and animals out of the Temple. He tipped over the tables, and money scattered everywhere. He tossed the chairs being used by those who sold doves, the cheapest creatures for sale. He turned to the moneychangers, his eyes blazing, and said, "The Scriptures [Holy Writings] declare, 'My Temple will be called a house of prayer,' but you have turned it into a den of thieves!" (Matthew 21:13).

Jesus cleared the area so people could come to him. He began healing the blind, and the lame, and those who were sick.

The religious leaders were furious. "The children are shouting, 'Praise God for the Son of David!' This is intolerable. Jesus!" they said. "Are you listening to what the children are saying? Make them stop!" They knew the children were welcoming Jesus as their Messiah.

"Yes, I hear them," Jesus said. But he did not make the children stop singing his praises. He reminded the religious leaders the Scriptures had foretold this event. Then he went back to healing people and teaching them.

That evening when Jesus left Jerusalem and went back to Bethany, the religious leaders met together. They tried to figure out a way to kill Jesus. But he was so popular. The people would surely rebel. They had to stop him somehow, but they didn't know what they could do. They were angry and frustrated. They couldn't stop Jesus.

FOOD FOR THOUGHT

Jesus showed his disciples and the people of Jerusalem he loved all people, including the non—Jewish visitors, when he cleared the temple for them. He put such a high value on prayer—communication with God—he was willing to bring the wrath of the religious leaders on himself to make his point.

Prayer is talking with God. Because of Jesus, we can come to God and express what is in our hearts. We do not have to speak fancy words or put everything just right. All we need to do is open our hearts to God and tell him we want to belong to him. He will always hear that prayer and answer, "Yes. Come to me."

CHAPTER 20—JESUS SERVES HIS DISCIPLES

The time was Passover week in Jerusalem. We are told Satan entered Judas Iscariot, one of the disciples. Judas went to the chief priests, the top religious leaders. He said, "How much will you give me if I arrange to hand Jesus over to you?"

The chief priests gave him thirty pieces of silver—the equivalent of pay for one hundred twenty days of work.

Judas tucked the money away and returned to the other disciples and Jesus.

"Lord, where do you want to celebrate the Passover feast?" the disciples asked.

Jesus told them where they could rent an upstairs room from a local man, probably one of Jesus's followers.

The disciples rented the room and bought what was needed for the feast.

That evening, Jesus and his disciples went to the room together. The disciples did not realize Jesus was going to be killed soon. They had been arguing from time to time among themselves, even during Passover, about who would be the greatest in Jesus's coming kingdom.

When they reached the room, they were hot and dusty. As they sat down, Jesus took off his robe and tied a towel around his waist. He filled a big bowl with water and headed back to the disciples. He knelt before one of the men, lifted his feet, washed off the dust, then dried them.

The disciples were horrified. Jesus? Washing their feet? That was the job of a servant.

Jesus came to Peter with the water. But Peter wasn't having any part of this. "No!" he exclaimed. "You will not wash my feet."

Jesus said, "Peter, if you do not let me wash your feet, you won't belong to me."

Peter looked at Jesus for a moment. "Then wash my hands—wash my head, too. Don't just wash my feet, Lord."

Jesus said, "Someone who has already bathed doesn't need to be washed all over. Just his feet need to be washed. You and the other disciples are clean—except for one of you." Jesus knew what Judas Iscariot had done.

When he had finished washing their feet, Jesus put his robe on again and rejoined them at the table. He asked, "Do you understand what I was doing? You call me 'Teacher' and 'Lord,' and you are right, because that's what I am. And since I, your Lord and Teacher, have washed your feet, you ought to wash each other's feet. I have given you an example to follow. Do as I have done to you. I tell you the truth, slaves are not greater than their master. Nor is the messenger more important than the one who sends the message. Now that you know these things, God will bless you for doing them" (John 13:12—17).

Jesus was teaching them that those who want to be great in his kingdom must be servants of all, not lording it over others. He set the example. He was God the Son, and he demonstrated humility by taking on the role of a servant and washing their dirty feet.

FOOD FOR THOUGHT

I recently worked for a year with a group of elementary and junior high students, teaching them how to serve others. At first, they resisted. Gradually, they began asking others how they could help them. Some of the students began doing more and more for others. At the end of the year, two of them told me, "You know, I discovered helping others makes me feel good!"

They learned the joy of serving others. Is there someone in your world who needs help? Have you considered reaching out to help them?

CHAPTER 21—THE LORD'S SUPPER

The same night that Jesus washed his disciples' feet, they all sat down to eat the Passover feast together. The feast was of roasted lamb, flat (unleavened) bread, an herbal dipping sauce for the bread, and red wine.

While they were eating, Jesus said, "One of you will betray me."

The disciples were stunned. They began asking, "Am I the one? I could never do that."

Jesus said, "It is one who dips his bread into the bowl with me."

In those days, sharing a meal together meant people were safe with the other people sharing their meal. It was their custom. One did not expect to be harmed by someone who shared a meal. To harm such a one was considered a terrible betrayal. Jesus was clear about what he said—the betrayal would come from one of those twelve men who ate with him that night.

The disciples were horrified. They asked, "Is it me?"

Sometime during the meal or right after it, Jesus looked at Judas, knowing what was in his heart, and said, "Go. Do what you are going to do."

The others thought Jesus was sending Judas on an errand. But Jesus knew he was sending Judas to the chief priests, where he would betray his Lord.

Jesus held up a piece of flat bread. He gave thanks to God for the bread then said to his remaining disciples, "Here is the bread. Eat it. This bread is my body, which is to be broken for you."

The disciples were stunned. What did Jesus mean?

Then Jesus held up his cup of wine and told his disciples to drink it. "Drink from this cup. It is my blood. It is the new covenant between God and man."

In those days, contracts—covenants—were sealed by blood, by sacrifices. The first covenant between God and Abraham was sealed by an animal sacrifice. Now Jesus was making a new covenant with the people of earth, and the blood sacrifice would be his own body. The new covenant would replace the old covenant and would bring forgiveness of sins for all who believed in him.

"My blood will be poured out for many so their sins will be forgiven. I won't drink wine again until we drink it together in my Father's kingdom."

The disciples silently drank from the cup. Whatever did Jesus mean?

Maybe Andrew remembered the words of John the Baptist and wondered, for John had said, "Look! The Lamb of God who takes away the sins of the world." But he did not know at the time what John meant.

Jesus told them, "I'm giving you a new command—Love each other the same way I have loved you. This is how the world will know that you are my disciples."

After they had finished eating, they sang a song about God together. It may have been an old Passover song entitled "Dayenu." That word means, "It would have been enough for us." The song recounts the story of God delivering the nation of Israel from slavery in Egypt and leading them to the land of Canaan. It is still a popular Passover song today.

Like many others do, the disciples took a walk together after dinner. They walked outside the city to the Garden of Gethsemane, one of Jesus's favorite places. On the way, Jesus said, "Tonight, you will all desert me."

Peter said, "No! Even if all the rest desert you, I will not!"

Jesus said, "Peter, before the rooster crows in the morning, you will deny me three times, and say you don't know me."

"No!" Peter insisted. All the others said the same thing.

When they arrived at the garden, Jesus told most of his disciples to stay in a certain place while he went to another part of the garden to pray. He took Peter and Zebedee's two sons, James and John, a little farther.

Knowing what lay ahead of him, Jesus asked his closest disciples, Peter, James, and John, to come stay in an area near him, while he went on to pray. He told them, "I am weighed down with great sorrow. Face this struggle with me. Pray with me"

Jesus was stricken with grief, knowing what would be done to him. He had begged his disciples to pray. But the three disciples were sleepy and full, and they fell asleep. They didn't know what was coming.

Jesus, alone in another part of the garden, cried out to his Father. "My Father! If it is possible, let this cup of suffering be taken away from me. Yet I want your will to be done, not mine" (Matthew 26:39).

Twice Jesus went back to his disciples and found them asleep. "Couldn't you pray with me for even one hour?" he asked. "Please. Pray with me. I do not want you to fall into temptation."

The third time Jesus returned and found them asleep, he let them be. He turned and went back to pray alone. When he returned, Jesus woke them. "It's time. I am going to be betrayed now. Look! Here comes the one who will betray me."

A big crowd of men armed with clubs and swords came toward Jesus. In the front of this mob came Judas. He walked up to Jesus. "Greetings, Jesus," he said and kissed him on the cheek. A kiss was the signal he had arranged so the crowd would know which one was Jesus.

The crowd with Judas grabbed Jesus. "We're arresting you!" they declared.

Peter drew his sword to try to rescue his teacher. He swung it through the air and cut off the ear of the high priest's servant, Malchus.

"No," Jesus said. "Men who use the sword will die by it. Don't you know that I could have asked my Father for twelve legions of angels to rescue me?" Twelve legions can be up to seventy–two thousand. "But I didn't call them. This is supposed to happen to me." He reached out and touched Malchus's ear, and it was healed.

I have wondered whether Malchus's life was changed in that moment of healing. Did he suddenly realize who Jesus was? Did he later follow Jesus? The Bible does not say. But in that moment when others were trying to harm Jesus, our Lord gave that man grace and healing. Malchus must have been impacted tremendously.

The mob took Jesus back to the religious leaders. The leading priests and the high council put Jesus through a mock trial with false witnesses who couldn't even agree with each other.

Jesus remained silent.

This frustrated the high priest immensely. He couldn't rattle Jesus at all. Finally, he said, "'I demand in the name of the living God—tell us if you are the Messiah, the Son of God.'

"Jesus replied, 'You have said it. And in the future you will see the Son of Man seated in the place of power at God's right hand and coming on the clouds of heaven'" (Matthew 26:63–64).

The high priest ripped his robe apart to show how horrified he pretended to be. He shouted, "Blasphemy! We don't need any other witnesses!" He turned to the crowd and said, "What verdict to you say?"

The crowd shouted, "Guilty! He should die!"

They spit on Jesus's face and beat him up. Some slapped him. They all mocked Jesus.

Peter was brave enough to follow where the mob had taken Jesus. He was outside in the courtyard. One of the high priest's servant girls went up to him and asked, "Weren't you with Jesus in Galilee?"

But Peter said, "What are you talking about? Of course not! I don't even know the man!"

Three times that night, people came up to Peter and said, "Say, don't we know you? You're one of Jesus's disciples!" But Peter denied knowing Jesus.

At dawn, a rooster crowed. Suddenly, Peter remembered what Jesus had said. He turned and ran away, crying bitterly because he had failed his Lord.

FOOD FOR THOUGHT

Peter failed. He denied he even knew Jesus, the one who had allowed him to walk on water, the one who had fed the multitudes, the one who loved people, healed them, and forgave their sins. Words cannot describe how badly Peter felt. Have you ever felt that you have failed God big time? If you have, you know something of what Peter felt that day.

But Jesus loved Peter. He was not finished with him. Jesus had a plan to restore Peter once again. No failure of ours can separate us from God's love. Jesus loves us, even when we fail him. Remember, Jesus said those who are forgiven much, will love much. God values your love more than you can imagine. He will forgive you if you fail, if you ask him.

CHAPTER 22—THE CRUCIFIXION

The story of what happened to Jesus next can be found in all four books of the Bible known as The Gospels—Matthew, Mark, Luke, and John. (See Reference section). I will combine these accounts and mention the main things that happened.

The religious leaders sent Jesus to Pontius Pilate, the Roman governor, for sentencing. The Jews could have stoned Jesus, as they tried earlier, but they could not have Jesus crucified. They wanted Jesus to be crucified—it was the most humiliating death imaginable—and they hated him passionately. But only the Romans were authorized to crucify people.

Pilate didn't want to be caught in the middle of this. He knew how popular Jesus was. He sent Jesus over to Herod, the king of Judea. "This is a Jewish problem, not mine," he declared.

Herod asked Jesus some questions. He had heard a lot about Jesus, and he relished the chance to talk to him. But Jesus refused to answer. The religious leaders told Herod their complaint. Herod and his soldiers mocked Jesus. Finally, they put a purple robe on him—a robe like kings wore—and sent him back to Pilate.

The chief priests were demanding Jesus be executed—crucified. They said he was guilty under Jewish law. It was up to Pilate to sentence Jesus. Pilate said, "If you want to execute him, go ahead."

"We don't have the authority to crucify him. Only you do," they answered.

Pilate talked with Jesus in private. He, too, had heard stories about Jesus. "Are you the King of the Jews?" he asked.

Jesus looked at Pilate and said, "You have said it. My kingdom is not of this world. It is somewhere else. If it were here, my servants would have prevented this. I was sent here to earth to give witness to the truth. Those who love truth listen to me."

Pilate said cynically, "What is truth?"

He stood up and led Jesus back to the mob and priests. He knew the Jews wanted Jesus killed because they were jealous of him. As he sat down on the judgment seat, he received a message from his wife. She wrote, "Don't have anything to do with this innocent man. I had an awful dream about him during the night."

Pilate told the religious leaders, "You brought Jesus to me saying he had started a revolt. I have spoken with this man, Jesus, and he is innocent. I find no fault in this man," he said. "It is the custom for me to release one prisoner to you a year. So I ask you, do you want me to release Jesus, the King of the Jews, or Barabbas, a rebel and a murderer?"

The crowd shouted, "Give us Barabbas! Give us Barabbas!"

Pilate had Jesus beaten by the Roman soldiers, who mocked him and taunted him. They put the purple robe over him. They shoved a crown of long, sharp thorns down on Jesus's head. The prophet Isaiah tells us Jesus's face was disfigured by the time they finished tormenting him.

Bloody from the beating, Jesus was taken back to the crowd. "Look at this man! He is innocent!" Pilate said. He tried to get the Jews to release Jesus.

But the crowd shouted, "If you don't execute him, you are no friend of the emperor, Caesar!" That was a serious charge. If those words got back to Caesar, Pilate would be in trouble.

"What should I do with Jesus who is called the Messiah?" Pilate demanded.

"Crucify him! Crucify him! Crucify him!" the mob chanted viciously.

Pilate had a servant bring out a bowl of water. In front of the crowd, he said, "I wash my hands of this man's blood. I am innocent of this death. I want nothing to do with this."

"Let his blood be on us ... and on our children!" the mob shouted.

Pilate then sentenced Jesus to be crucified. But he ordered a sign to be nailed on the cross above him which said, "King of the Jews." He had it written in Aramaic, Latin, and Greek so all could read it.

The soldiers placed the crossbeam of the cross on Jesus's bloody shoulders and led him out toward the place where he would be crucified. It was a hill outside Jerusalem called "Golgotha" or "the place of the skull."

On the way out of the city, Jesus stumbled from his weakness at being beaten. He could not get up again. The crossbeam held him down. The soldiers grabbed a man out of the crowd, Simon of Cyrene, and made him carry the crossbeam for Jesus.

When they reached the hill, the soldiers laid Jesus on the cross and nailed his hands and feet to it with great, iron spikes. Then they hoisted the cross up. They dropped the cross into the hole dug for it.

Jesus prayed aloud for the Roman soldiers. "Father, forgive them! They do not know what they are doing!" These men came from a foreign land and a foreign religion. They knew nothing about the one, true God. They knew nothing about the Messiah. They did not know they were killing the Son of God. Jesus wanted his Father to forgive them. He came to earth to die for their sins, too. Jesus loved them!

The religious leaders protested when the Roman soldiers put up the sign that read, "King of the Jews." They ran back to Pilate and told him, "Take that sign down!"

But Pilate was firm. "The sign stays."

On each side of Jesus, the soldiers crucified two convicted thieves. There the three men hung, struggling to breathe, pain shooting throughout their bodies.

Below Jesus's cross, the chief priests and religious leaders walked, mocking him. "You saved others, but you can't save yourself!"

But Jesus did not respond to their tormenting words.

One of the thieves who had been crucified next to Jesus, jeered at him too. He said, "So you're the Messiah, are you? Prove it by saving yourself—and us, too, while you're at it!"

But the other thief said, "'Don't you fear God even when you have been sentenced to die? We deserve to die for our crimes, but this man hasn't done anything wrong.' Then he said, 'Jesus, remember me when you come into your kingdom'" Luke 23:40—43).

Jesus replied, "I assure you, today you will be with me in paradise."

John was the only one of Jesus's twelve disciples who followed him to Golgotha and stood near the cross. He was comforting Mary, Jesus's mother. Jesus said to John, "This is now your mother." To Mary, Jesus said, "This is your son." He wanted John to look after Mary when he was gone. From then on, John took care of Mary for Jesus.

Mary's sister, whose name may have been Salome, together with Mary Magdalene and Mary the wife of Cleopas, were all huddled close to Jesus's mother too. These four women and John were brave enough to stay close to Jesus in his time of great pain and sorrow.

The sky grew dark around noon and stayed dark until about three o'clock. People became nervous. While he hung there on the cross, Jesus cried out, "Eloi, Eloi, lema sabachthani?" meaning, "My God, my God, why have you abandoned me?"

No one else understood that God had placed the sins of the world on Jesus at Golgotha. Jesus was the perfect lamb, sacrificed for the sins of the world. He was covered symbolically with every wicked act, every filthy word, and every human failure, both large and small, which humanity had ever committed or ever would commit. He became sin— for us.

God turned his face away from his Son and poured out his wrath against sin. For the first time in eternity, God the Father and God the Holy Spirit were spiritually separated from God the Son. The separation from the Father and Spirit was a crushing blow to God the Son. Jesus's heart was broken.

Then Jesus shouted with a loud voice, "It is finished!"

The work Jesus had come to do was complete. He had paid the price for our sins through his own death for us, in our place.

"Jesus shouted, 'Father, I entrust my spirit into your hands!' And with those words he breathed his last" (Luke 23:46)

These were not the shouts of a tortured, exhausted man. They were shouts of strength and victory.

The earth shook violently. The very rocks of Golgotha were torn apart. People were terrified.

The Roman officer who was in charge of the crucifixion said, "This man was definitely innocent—he was surely the Son of God!" Luke tells us the soldier worshipped God at that moment. He may have been the first non–Jew to believe in Jesus.

In Jerusalem, the curtain in the Temple was suddenly torn down the middle, from top to bottom. Before that time, the curtain kept everyone but the high priest from coming into God's presence. Now the curtain was ripped apart. This was how God let the world know that now everyone could come into his presence because of what Jesus had just done.

While Satan and his demons shouted with glee at their success in killing the Son of God, they did not realize Jesus had just defeated them. Jesus had delivered a deathblow to Satan, and the devil didn't even understand what had happened.

Remember? God's first clue about the Promised One was this—the serpent (Satan) would bruise the heel of the Promised One. But the Promised One would crush the serpent's head. That happened at Golgotha. Satan may have killed Jesus's body, but Jesus defeated Satan forever that day. For he made a way to free humanity from the sin trap. Satan didn't even know he was defeated—yet.

FOOD FOR THOUGHT

Remember the sin trap illustration? If you chose to participate in this illustration, you put your name or photo inside a container and put a lid on it. Here's what happened at Golgotha. When Jesus died that day, he gained authority over the sin trap. Satan no longer has complete control over it. When you give your life to Jesus and ask to be rescued from sin, Jesus tells Satan, "This person (put your name here) has given me their life. I paid the price to free them from the sin trap. Satan, you no longer have authority over (your name). I am taking (your name) out of the sin trap." Jesus then opens the trap, takes you out of it, and closes the lid behind you.

Would you like to be free from sin and belong to Jesus, who loves you so much that he died for you? Then let's make this real for you. Look at the picture of Jesus on the cross right now

Think of hurtful or prideful things you have done, things you know are wrong. God calls it sin. Confess to God the wrong things you've done. Name the things as they come to your mind. With a pencil, scribble a mark (or several marks) on Jesus's body. Or you can write the sins on the picture of Jesus. Imagine those marks are your sins, and you are transferring them to Jesus on the cross. For that's what happened at Golgotha. Jesus took on himself the punishment for your sins, for my sins, and for the sins of all humanity as he hung on the cross. If you would like to receive God's forgiveness, which has been offered to you through Jesus, pray this prayer.

"Father God in heaven, thank you for sending your Son, Jesus, to earth to pay the penalty for my sins. I confess to you I am a sinner and cannot rescue myself from my own nature to do wrong things. I ask you to come into my heart—my life— and forgive me for my sins. I ask you to make my heart clean inside. I want to follow Jesus from this moment forward. I give you my life now. Amen."

If you put your name or photo inside the sin trap earlier, open the trap now, take your name/photo out, and close the lid.

Jesus said, "If the Son sets you free, you are truly free" (John 8:36).

Jim Elliot, a missionary who gave his life in an attempt to take the good news about Jesus to a primitive tribe in the jungles of Ecuador, wrote this in his journal on October 28, 1949. "He is no fool who gives what he cannot keep to gain that which he cannot lose."[1]

Jim Elliot lost his earthly life, but he gained eternal life with God in heaven because of his choice to follow Jesus. Our lives on earth are short. Eternity is certain.

CHAPTER 23—THE RESURRECTION

The complete work of Jesus did not end the day he died on the cross. His disciples didn't know that. They were frightened and crushed in spirit.

Judas Iscariot had been so upset he had tried to stop the trial of Jesus. He went back to the chief priests and tried to give the money back to them. They refused to take the silver pieces. Judas went out and hanged himself in remorse for what he had done.

When Jesus died, the earthquake God sent was so fierce many tombs were opened around the city. Many people of Jerusalem who had loved God during their lifetime were raised from the dead and left their graves. After Jesus's resurrection, they walked around Jerusalem for everyone to see. Can you imagine what a shock that must have been?

The Jewish leaders didn't let the earthquake or anything else stop them in their own pursuits. They wanted to get the crucified men off those crosses before sunset, before the Sabbath day started. They had the Roman soldiers break the legs of the two thieves. This prevented them from breathing. They died within moments. When the soldiers came to Jesus, they could see he was probably dead, but just to be sure, one of them thrust a spear into his body. Blood and water came from his side, showing he had been dead for some time.

Nicodemus, one of the religious leaders who secretly believed in Jesus, and another disciple, Joseph of Arimathea, a rich man, took Jesus's body away and put it in Joseph's family tomb. They wrapped Jesus's body lightly, because there was no time to do more, and they put a cloth over his face. The two men rolled the heavy stone across the tomb's opening. They took seventy–five pounds of spices to use in preparing Jesus's body. We do not know if they had enough time to prepare the body properly for burial, for the Sabbath was about to start We do know they at least got a start on it. The Sabbath was a day of rest and worship, which lasted from sundown on Friday to sundown on Saturday each week. On that day, no one was allowed to do any work.

On Saturday, the day after Jesus died, the religious leaders went to see Pilate. "This man, Jesus, claimed he would rise again on the third day. We want you to put a heavy guard around his tomb, so his disciples won't come and steal his body, then claim he rose from the dead!"

"Go ahead. Take a guard," Pilate said.

The religious leaders sent Roman soldiers out to the tomb. The soldiers put a seal on the grave and guarded it. They were under orders to make sure Jesus's body stayed there.

The disciples of Jesus went back to the room they had rented. There they grieved together, uncertain what to do next. Sabbath passed. Very early on Sunday morning, some of the women who followed Jesus took spices and more wrappings to the tomb to prepare his body properly for burial. The women were Mary Magdalene, Mary, the mother of James, and Salome.

When the women arrived at the tomb, there was a violent earthquake. An angel of the Lord came down from heaven and rolled away the stone, then sat on it. He was bright like lightning. His clothes were pure white. The guards were terrified. They shook and fell like dead men.

The angel told the women, "Don't be afraid. Jesus, who was crucified, is not here. He has risen, just like he said. Come. Look inside the tomb and see where he was laid. Then run back and tell his disciples Jesus is alive, and he will meet them in Galilee."

The women saw the empty tomb. The angel had frightened them tremendously, so some went back to their homes instead of telling the disciples. Mary Magdalene, however, ran back to the room where the disciples were gathered and told them what had just happened. The men did not believe her. They probably suggested to Mary that someone had moved Jesus's body.

Peter and John decided to check it out. They ran toward the tomb, which was in a garden. The Roman guards had fled by then, and the tomb was open. John arrived first. He saw the strips of linen that had been wrapped around Jesus's body. Jesus wasn't inside the cocoon of cloth. They saw the linen cloth that had been over Jesus face. The cloth was folded and set aside. John believed then Jesus had risen from the dead. Peter still wasn't sure. They went back to the other disciples and told what they had seen.

Mary Magdalene was no longer sure about what had happened. The weekend had been traumatic. She had watched Jesus die on the cross. She had seen the soldiers thrust a spear into his side. She had seen an angel who had said Jesus was alive. But the disciples didn't believe her. Maybe they were right. She was confused. She went back to the tomb, tears running down her cheeks. She bent down and craned her neck to look into the grave.

Two angels sat inside. They asked, "Why are you crying?"

"They have taken my Lord's body away from here, and I don't know where they have put him," she said.

Mary turned around to walk away. A man standing there asked, "Why are you crying?"

Mary, blinded by tears, thought he was the gardener. Maybe he would know. "If you have taken my Lord's body away, would you please tell me where he is? I'll go get him."

The man said, "Mary."

Then she recognized him. He was Jesus. "Teacher!" she gasped.

She must have started to hug him, for Jesus said, "No, don't hold onto me. I still have to go to my Father. What I want you to do is this—Go tell my disciples I'm returning to my Father and yours."

Mary went back to the disciples. She told them, "I have seen the Lord!"

Later, Jesus appeared to all his disciples. The Bible tells us Jesus remained in Judea for forty days, and about five hundred people saw him after he rose from the dead.

Peter went back to his home beside the Sea of Galilee. He was discouraged. Even if Jesus was alive, Peter had denied knowing him during his trial. Peter felt awful. How could he have done that? Could Jesus ever forgive him?

Several other disciples went back to Galilee too. They went fishing one night. By morning, they had caught nothing, so they started back home. As they were nearing the shoreline, they saw a man standing there.

The man called, "Have you caught any fish?"

"No," they shouted back.

"Well, throw your net out on the right side of your boat. You'll catch fish there."

They did. Suddenly, the fishing net was weighed down with so many fish the men were not able to haul the net back in.

John immediately knew who the man on the shore was. He'd seen this same kind of miracle before. "Peter," he said, leaning over, "it's the Lord!"

Peter jumped out of the boat and swam toward the shore. He raced up to Jesus. The other disciples dragged the net along with them toward the shore. When they arrived, they found Jesus had made a fire and was cooking fish over it. Together, they sat around the fire and ate breakfast.

Afterward, Jesus had a talk with Peter. "Peter, do you truly love me?"

Peter said, "Yes, Lord. You know I do."

"Then feed my lambs," Jesus said, referring to the children who believed in him.

Jesus asked Peter two more times if he loved him. Both times, Peter said, "Yes." Both times, Jesus said, "Then feed my sheep." Peter was to teach the adults and lead them as well.

Peter, who had denied Jesus three times, was given three chances to reaffirm his love. Peter later became the leader of the other disciples, for Jesus would return to heaven soon.

FOOD FOR THOUGHT

Jesus is the God of second chances and more. We will all fail to live up to what we know is right at times. But Jesus is patient with us. He forgives our failures and sins when we ask for forgiveness.

The secret to a good, healthy relationship with God is confessing our sins quickly, asking for forgiveness, and trusting he will indeed forgive us. The Apostle John tells us, "But if we confess our sins to him, he is faithful and just to forgive us our sins and to cleanse us from all wickedness" (I John 1:9).

God forgives all who come to him through Jesus.

CHAPTER 24—THE PROMISE

For forty days, Jesus gave instructions to his disciples and friends. He told them what they should do next. One thing he told them was what to do immediately after he returned to heaven:

"Do not leave Jerusalem until the Father sends you the gift he promised, as I told you before. John baptized with water, but in just a few days you will be baptized with the Holy Spirit."

The day came when Jesus was to leave the earth and return to heaven. He told his remaining eleven disciples to meet him on a mountain in Galilee. When they saw Jesus, they worshipped him.

Jesus's last words to them before leaving were, "I have been given all authority in heaven and on earth. Therefore, go and make disciples of all the nations, baptizing them in the name of the Father and the Son and the Holy Spirit. Teach these new disciples to obey all the commands I have given you. And be sure of this: I am with you always, even to the end of the age" (Matthew 28:18–20). This is known as "The Great Commission" given to Christians.

With that, Jesus began to rise into the air. He disappeared into the clouds. He now sits at the right hand of God the Father. When Satan tries to accuse Christians of sin, Jesus reminds the Father of his sacrifice for us, and claims us as his own. We are forgiven.

Jesus said he will return to earth someday. He also said, at the end of the age, many will claim to be him and will do many signs and wonders. The way to know if a person is really Jesus is this. He will return to earth from the sky—from the clouds—in the same way he left the earth. He will come with a mighty shout and with tens of thousands of those who believed in him during their lifetimes. There will be no mistaking that he is Jesus. He promised he will return to earth for us, to establish his kingdom over the entire planet.

The Apostle Paul wrote about Jesus's return to earth.

"We tell you this directly from the Lord: We who are still living when the Lord returns will not meet him ahead of those who have died. For the Lord himself will come down from heaven with a commanding shout, and with the voice of the archangel, and with the trumpet call of God. First, the Christians who have died will rise from their graves. Then, together with them, we who are still alive and remain on the earth will be caught up in the clouds to meet the Lord in the air. Then we will be with the Lord forever. So encourage each other with these words" (1 Thessalonians 4:15—18).

The disciples returned to Jerusalem and waited for the gift of the Holy Spirit. They prayed and kept focused on Jesus. Ten days after Jesus returned to heaven, when they were together praying, God the Holy Spirit came into the room with the sound of a mighty, rushing wind. Bright flames of what looked like tongues of fire came down, separated, and rested on each of them. They all began to speak in different languages, in the power of the Holy Spirit.

All the people in Jerusalem, and those who had come from far away nations, were able to hear the good news about Jesus in their own language. This happened fifty days after Jesus rose from the dead. That day is called "Pentecost," and was only the beginning of the mighty work God began doing on earth through the Holy Spirit, and through those who believe in Jesus and follow him.

Some may wonder why Jesus did not fully rescue humanity from Satan after the resurrection. Why do we still live with sin's power and temptations threatening to overcome us? When will we be completely free from Satan's power? When will the rescue plan be finished?

The best comparison of how it works is this. When we have an election in the United States, we vote in November. But the winners do not take office until January. The losers have some authority until the winners are sworn in. We're living between the time when Jesus won the battle for planet Earth and the day when Jesus will claim his kingdom as King of Kings, and Lord of Lords. At that point, the rescue plan will be complete. In the meantime, we have to endure Satan's limited, "lame duck" rule on this planet.

When Jesus returns as King, he will remove Satan from power. All who have believed in Jesus will finally be free from sin and death. The rescue plan will be complete.

We do not know when Jesus will return to earth, but prophecies in the Bible indicate he will return in the near future. One of the early prophetic signs was the nation of Israel being scattered throughout the whole earth. Jesus said the Temple would not have one stone standing on top of another when Jerusalem was destroyed. That was the first prophecy about Israel's future. That happened in 70 A.D. when the Romans invaded. Ten tribes of Israel had already been scattered, leaving the tribes of Levi and Judah in the part of the land known as Judea. Titus, the leader of the Roman army, dismantled Jerusalem and scattered the inhabitants of Judea. This set the stage for another prophecy that would happen much later.

The second prophecy, the one which will happen shortly before Jesus's return to earth, would be the return of the Hebrews to their homeland, Israel. After nearly two thousand years of being scattered, the Hebrews began returning to their homeland before World War II. They became a nation again in 1948.

Jesus gave us a third prophecy. The good news about what he did for mankind by dying for their sins would be told throughout the entire world just before he would return. At this time, the story of Jesus and what he did for us has been told among almost all people groups on earth.

The Apostle Paul said this about why there is such a long gap between the time Jesus won the battle for earth and when he will return. "The Lord isn't really being slow about his promise, as some people think. No, he is being patient for your sake. He does not want anyone to be destroyed, but wants everyone to repent" (2 Peter 3:9).

From eternity, *God* saw our generation. He loved us from eternity and holds out his hands, inviting us to love him back. Inviting us to believe in him. Inviting us to become his own children, so he can shower on us the rich blessings he has stored up for us in eternity. Jesus hasn't yet returned as King because he's been waiting for us. He's been waiting for *you*. If he had returned to planet Earth sooner, we would not have even existed.

While we wait for his return, we still struggle against our sinful natures. Even when our souls belong to Jesus, we will not be completely free from sin until we die and go to heaven or until Jesus comes back.

When Jesus returned to Heaven, he did not leave his followers without power. For those who believe in him, Jesus sent God the Holy Spirit to live in our hearts. The Holy Spirit teaches us what we need to know to live in a way pleasing to the Father. The Holy Spirit is our Teacher and Comforter. He gives us victory over sin.

The Holy Spirit develops the following character qualities in us—love, joy, peace, patience, kindness, goodness, faithfulness, gentleness, and self–control.

God has given us prayer as a powerful tool to reach others for Jesus, and to defeat the work of Satan.

Prayer is our most powerful weapon against Satan. If we try to do God's work without prayer, it's like trying to vacuum a floor without plugging the vacuum into the electricity. Or like trying to cut a tree down with a chain saw, but not turning on the motor. Prayer connects us to the power of God, so we can do the work of God. Prayer protects us from the schemes of Satan. Through prayer, God can and often does deliver miracles into people's lives.

We depend on the Holy Spirit to deliver messages to and from God. We should stay alert and be persistent in our prayers for other Christians, both here and in other parts of the world, as needs arise. Our prayers send God's power to help meet the needs of others too.

God has given us armor to protect us. The armor of God is awesome. The Apostle Paul calls it "the body armor of God's righteousness." This armor keeps us from slipping back into evil actions or thoughts. Here's what the whole armor of God is and what it does for us.

The Belt of Truth—Protects our hearts from the lies of Satan.

Armored Shoes—Keeps our foundation (our hearts and minds) at peace, reminds us Jesus rescued us from the power of sin when he died on the cross.

The Shield of Faith—Stops the fiery arrows of guilt and blame Satan shoots at our hearts.

The Helmet of Salvation—Reminds us we belong to Jesus, and Satan has no power over us.

The Sword of the Spirit—This is the Word of God. The Bible is God's Word. It is true.

When we follow Jesus's teachings, we become strong and can stand against any evil Satan plans for us. Prayer is part of receiving God's Word as well, for God speaks to us when we go to him for instructions. He puts impressions based on the Bible into our hearts to guide us. He nudges us to talk to certain people about Jesus. He warns us when we should not be part of something. He fills us with his presence and brings great joy to our hearts.

Paul also tells us to pray in the Holy Spirit all the time. Our hearts need to be connected with God always in order to use the armor of God most effectively. With these weapons, we can stand strong against the works of Satan. We can help others out of the sin trap by living in God's power and keeping our eyes on Jesus. We can make a difference in our world.

FOOD FOR THOUGHT

God wants us to share our faith with others. We are part of God's team to reach planet Earth with the life–saving message of Jesus. When we obey, we have this promise from the prophet Daniel—"Those who lead many to righteousness will shine like the stars forever."

Go out into your world now and live in the strength and power God has given you. As you go, hold onto these words of the Apostle Paul. "And I am convinced that nothing can ever separate us from God's love. Neither death nor life, neither angels nor demons, neither our fears for today nor our worries about tomorrow—not even the powers of hell can separate us from God's love. No power in the sky above or in the earth below—indeed, nothing in all creation will ever be able to separate us from the love of God that is revealed in Christ Jesus our Lord" (Romans 8: 38–39).

May the Lord hold you close to his heart always.

ABOUT THE AUTHOR

Sheri Schofield is a Bible teacher and award–winning author/illustrator, serving God in the Rocky Mountains of Montana, at Helena Alliance Church. Colorado Christian Writers' Conference named her Writer of the Year in 2018.

Sheri began teaching the Bible as a young teenager with Child Evangelism Fellowship. By the time she was fifteen, she was teaching her own Sunday school class of second–grade girls. During college, she studied theology and Christian education of children at Prairie Bible College and Biola University in preparation for her lifework.

After many years of teaching children about Jesus through her classes and books, Sheri now writes for adults as well. She is a member of Advanced Writers & Speakers Association (AWSA). Along with a great team of other writers at Arise Daily Devotions (arisedailydevos.wordpress.com), Sheri offers insights about God's work in our lives. She often brings her life among the wild creatures of Montana into her writing.

AWSA named her Arise Daily Devotions Writer of the Year in 2020.

Sheri is the president of *Faithwind 4 Kids* ministry, serving alongside Tim, her husband. The ministry's focus is to put her books about salvation into the hands of children, teens, and their parents.

"I see myself as a planter, throwing seeds out into a field. The books are the seeds. The people around me are the field. God waters the seeds, which grow in people's hearts and eventually become his harvest. My job is to plant the seeds of the gospel, then pray for God to work," Sheri says. "I want to do my part in helping others meet Jesus.

ENDNOTES

Chapter 1

1. Isaac Watts, "O God Our Help in Ages Past," *The Psalms of David Imitated in the Language of the New Testament* (1719).

Chapter 2

1. Illustra Media provides excellent, college level scientific evidence of a Creator at https://illustramedia.com. Answers in Genesis provides more easily understood material at www.answersingenesis.org.

Chapter 22

1. Elisabeth Elliot, (chapel message, Prairie Bible Institute, 1974)

REFERENCES

Introduction

Page 13—God lifts burdens Hebrews—Matthew 11:28

Page 14—Good has good plans for you—Jeremiah 29:11

Page 14—God placed eternity in your heart—Ecclesiastes 3:11; Matthew 22:31,32

Page 14—King David tells about God—Psalm 34:4; Psalm 139:17,18; Psalm 91:2; Jeremiah 29:13

Page 15—How great God's love for you is—Ephesians 3:18

CHAPTER 1—HOW IT ALL BEGAN

Page 16—God is a spirit—John 1:18

Page 16—The Bible is true—2 Timothy 3:16

Page 16—God is light—1 John 1:5

Page 16—God is three persons in one—Matthew 28:19; Isaiah 9:6

Page 17—Jesus is called the Word—John 1:1, 14–18

Page 17—Jesus is our high priest—Hebrews 7:23–29

Page 17—God the Holy Spirit is called the Comforter, or the Helper—John 14:26

Page 17—Dream about a rock torn from a mountain—Daniel 2:34,15

Page 17—God is good—1 Chronicles 16:34

Page 17—God is holy—Isaiah 6:3

Page 17—God's throne in heaven—Revelation 4:8

Page 18—God is merciful and just—Psalm 116:5

Page 18—God is powerful—Matthew 19:26; Psalm 115:3

Page 18—God looks out for those who love him—Romans 8:28

Page 18—God's throne and river of life coming to earth—Revelation 21:1–7

Page 18—God knows all about us—Psalm 139

CHAPTER 2—CREATION AND THE SPIRITUAL CONNECTION

Page 20—The story of Creation and the Garden of Eden can be found in Genesis 1–2.

Page 21– Adam and Eve wore no clothes Genesis 2:25

Page 21—Humans have souls—Genesis 2:7

Page 22—Satan's background- -Isaiah 14:12–15; Revelation 12:7,8

Page 23—King David longed for God—Psalm 42:1,2

CHAPTER 3—THE CHOICE

The story of Adam and Eve's choice is found in Genesis 3:1–13.

Page 25—Sin results in death—Romans 6:23

Page 25—Humanity is separated from God because of sin—Isaiah 59:2

Page 25—We have been born into slavery to sin—Romans 3:23; Romans 5:12; John 8:34

Page 26—Apart from Jesus, our hearts are full of evil—Galatians 5:19–21

Page 27—God planned a rescue before creating humanity—1 Peter 1:19–20

Page 27—God reaches out to us while we are caught in sin—Romans 5:8

CHAPTER 4—GOD PLANS A RESCUE

The result of sin and the first hint of God's rescue plan can be found in Genesis 3:14–24.

Page 31—The Promised One would be born of a virgin—Isaiah 7:14

Page 31—The Promised One would be born in Bethlehem—Micah 5:2

Page 31—The Promised One would be a great King, and a star would announce his birth—Numbers 24:15–20

Page 31—Prophecy of Messiah—Isaiah 9:6–7

Page 31—Satan is the god of this world—2 Corinthians 4:4

Page 31—Satan's goal is to kill, steal and destroy—John 10:10

Page 31—Satan will do his worst just before Christ returns, because he knows his time is short—Revelation 12:12

Page 31—All that is good and perfect comes from God our Creator—James 1:17

Page 31—God's discipline is for our good—Hebrews 12:10

CHAPTER 5—THE RESCUE BEGINS

This story is found in Matthew chapters 1 & 2, and Luke chapter 1.

Page 32—God does not measure time like humans do—1 Peter 3:8

Page 32—What angels look like—Daniel 10:4–6

Page 34—Jesus and God the Father are one—John 10:30; John 14:9

CHAPTER 10—A NEW KIND OF FISHERMEN

CHAPTER 12—LESSONS IN FAITH

CHAPTER 13—JESUS THE HEALER

CHAPTER 14—JESUS, LORD OF ALL CREATION

CHAPTER 15—A DAY IN JESUS' LIFE

These stories are found in Matthew chapter 14:1–33 and John 6:1–21.
Page 72—Jesus was familiar with grief and sorrow—Isaiah 53:3
Page 73—The boy who gave Jesus his lunch—John 6:9
Page 74—Peter walks on water with Jesus—Matthew 14:24–33

CHAPTER 16—JESUS TO THE RESCUE

Page 76—The Abrahamic Covenant—Genesis 12:1–3
Page 77— The story of the woman caught in adultery—John 8:1–11.
Chapter 17—Unconditional Love
This story of a father's love for his wayward son is found in Luke 15:11–31.
Page 81—All things are possible with God—Matthew 19:26

CHAPTER 18—JESUS AND LAZARUS

The story of Jesus and Lazarus and what happened afterward is found in John chapter 11.

CHAPTER 19—JESUS NEARS HIS FINAL WEEK

Page 87—The story of Jesus at Mary, Martha, and Lazarus's home is found in John 12:1–8.
Page 87—Mary of Bethany anoints Jesus—John 12:3–7.
Page 88—The story of the bronze serpent—Numbers 21:4–8
Page 91—Religious leaders demand the children's silence—Matthew 21:14–16

CHAPTER 20—JESUS SERVES HIS DISCIPLES

Page 92—Judas agrees to betray Jesus—Matthew 26:14–16; Mark 14:10; Luke 22:1–6
Page 92—The disciples argue about who will be greatest—Luke 22:24–27
Page 92—Jesus washes disciples' feet—John 13:1–11

CHAPTER 21—THE LORD'S SUPPER

The story of the Lord's Supper can be found in Matthew 26:17–30; Mark 14:12–26; Luke 22:7–38; John 13:1–17:26.
Page 94—Jesus seals a new covenant between God and humanity—Matthew 26:27–28; Mark 14:22–24; Luke 22:17–20;

Page 95—The contract between God and Abraham shows contracts sealed with blood sacrifices—Genesis chapter 15
Page 95—The new command—John 13:34,35
Page 95-98—The story of what happened in Gethsemane is found in Matthew 26:36-56; Mark 14:32-49; Luke 22:39-54; John 18:1-11.
Page 97—Peter cuts off a servant's ear—John 18:10,11
Page 98—Peter denies knowing Jesus —Matthew 26:69-75; Mark 14:66-72

CHAPTER 22—THE CRUCIFIXION

More about the fraudulent trial of Jesus can be found in Matthew 26:57-27:31; Mark 14:53-15:20; Luke 22:63-23:25; John 18:12-16.
Page 100—Pilate's wife warned him not to harm Jesus—Matthew 27:19
Page 100—Jesus's face was disfigured by the torture— Isaiah 52:13-15
Page 100—Pilate washed his hands of Jesus's blood—Matthew 27:24
Page 101—The place where Jesus was crucified—Matthew 27:33
Page 101—Simon of Cyrene carried the cross for Jesus—Matthew 27:32
Page 101—Jesus asks God to forgive the Roman soldiers who crucified him—Luke 23:34
Page 102—The women at the cross—Mark 15:40; John 19:25
Mary's sister was at the cross with her. The names are given in these two passages. One writer calls her "Mary's sister" the other calls her "Salome". Since only the four women and John were at the cross, it may be assumed Salome was the sister of Mary.
Page 102—Jesus cries out to God—Mark 15:34
Page 103—Jesus shouted "It is finished!"– John 19:30
Page 103—Roman soldier declares Jesus innocent (Luke 23:47) and the Son of God (Mark 15:39)
Page 103—The Temple's curtain torn in two—Mark 15:38; Luke 23:45

CHAPTER 23—THE RESURRECTION

The story of the resurrection can be found in Matthew 28:1–15; Mark 16:16:1–8; Luke 24:1–12; John 20:1–18

Page 107—Judas Iscariot hanged himself in remorse—Matthew 27:1–5

Page 107—Many of the dead in Jerusalem were raised—Matthew 52–53

Page 107—Jewish leaders asked Pilate to break legs of crucified men—John 19:31–37

Page 107—Nicodemus and Joseph took Jesus' body away—Matthew 27:57–61; Mark 15:42–47; Luke 23:50–54; John 19:38–42

Page 108—Religious leaders demand a guard for Jesus's tomb—Matthew 27:62–66

Page 108—An angel appears at Jesus's empty tomb—Matthew 28:1–10; Mark 16:1–8; Luke 24:1–12; John 12:11,12

Page 109—Peter and John check on Jesus's empty tomb—Luke 24:12; John 20:3–10

Page 109—Jesus appears to Mary Magdalene—John 20:11–18

Page 110—Jesus was seen after resurrection by over 500 followers—1 Corinthians 15:5–6

Page 110—Jesus appears in Galilee to disciples—John 21:1–25

CHAPTER 24—THE PROMISE

Page 112—Promise of the Holy Spirit—Acts 1:4–5; Luke 24:49; John 14:15–26

Page 112—Jesus's last meeting with his disciples—Matthew 28:16–20

Page 112—Jesus returns to Heaven—Acts 1:9–11; Mark 16:19–20; Luke 24:50–53

Page 112—What Jesus is doing now—Hebrews chapter 8; Colossians 3:1

Page 112—Jesus promises to return to earth someday—Matthew 24:3 –35; Mark 13:3–37; Luke 21:7–36; John 14:1–4

Page 113—Paul describes what will happen when Jesus returns—1 Thessalonians 4:15–18 (NLT)

Page 113—The Holy Spirit is given to the Christians—Acts 2:1–41

Page 114—Jesus will remove Satan from power—Revelation chapter 20

Made in the USA
Middletown, DE
21 February 2022

61544453R00080